Table of Contents

Customs and Border Protection (CBP).. 1

   CBP INFO Center Self Service Q&A Database 1

   National Gang Intelligence Center (NGIC) 1

   CBP Border Community Liaison (BCL) Program 1

   CBP Information Center 2

   CBP State, Local & Tribal Liaison (SLT) 2

   CBP Tip Line 2

Civil Rights and Civil Liberties (CRCL)... 3

   Civil Rights Requirements in Federally Assisted Programs 3

   Community Roundtables 3

   CRCL Impact Assessments 4

   CRCL Newsletter.. 4

   CRCL Facebook Page 4

   Equal Employment Opportunity (EEO) Reports.. 4

   E-Verify and Unfair Labor Practices Training 4

   Forced Labor Resources 5

   How to File and Submit a Complaint 5

   Human Rights and Vulnerable Populations 5

   Human Rights Violators and War Crimes Unit 5

   Privacy, Civil Rights and Civil Liberties Fusion Center Training Program 5

   Quarterly NGO Civil Rights/Civil Liberties Committee Meetings... 6

   Office for Civil Rights and Civil Liberties (CRCL) Quarterly and Annual Reports to Congress 6

Office of Cybersecurity and Communications (CS&C) 7

   Multi-State Information Sharing and Analysis Center (MS-ISAC) 7

   Critical Infrastructure Partnership Advisory Council (CIPAC)... 7

   Information Technology-Government Coordinating Council (IT-GCC) 7

   Cyber Security Evaluation Tool (CSET) 8

   Cybersecurity Assessment and Risk Management Approach (CARMA) 8

   Software Assurance Forum 8

   "Build Security In" BSI 8

CyberStorm Exercise Series 8

National Cybersecurity Communications Integration Center (NCCIC) 8

United States Computer Emergency Readiness Team (US-CERT) 9

National Cyber Alert System (NCAS) 9

Industrial Control Systems Cyber Emergency Response Team (ICS-CERT)........................ 9

National Cyber Security Awareness Month and Stop.Think.Connect Campaign 9

Government Forum of Incident Response and Security (GFIRST) 10

Domestic Nuclear Detection Office (DNDO)... **11**

Radiological /Nuclear Detection and Adjudication Capability Development Framework (CDF) 11

National Incident Management System (NIMS) Preventive Radioactive/Nuclear Detection Resource
(PRND) Type Definitions 11

Training 11

Exercises... 12

Joint Analysis Center (JAC) 12

Federal Emergency Management Agency (FEMA) **13**

Community Emergency Response Team (CERT) 13

DisasterAssistance.gov.. 13

Emergency Management Institute Programs (EMI) 13

Flood Map Assistance Center (FMAC) 13

Private Sector E-alert 14

Incident Command System (ICS)... 14

Map Modernization Management Support (MMMS) 14

National Flood Insurance Program (NFIP) 15

National Incident Management System (NIMS) 15

National Response Framework (NRF) 15

National Training and Education Division (NTED)... 15

Ready Indian Country 16

Emergency Lodging Assistance Program 16

Voluntary Private Sector Preparedness Accreditation and Certification Program (PS-Prep)................. 16

Tornado Safety Initiative 16

U.S. Fire Administration's National Fire Academy (NFA) Training Programs 17

U.S. Fire Administration Publications 17

National Continuity Programs (NCP) 17

Federal Law Enforcement Training Centers (FLETC) **18**

Leadership and International Capacity Building Division / Leadership Institute Branch 18

Office of State, Local, Rural, Tribal and Territorial Training (SLRTT) 18

Office of Intelligence and Analysis (I&A) **20**

Alternative Analysis Workshop 20

Basic Intelligence and Threat Analysis Course 20

Clearance Nominations 20

Critical Thinking and Analytic Methods Course 20

Homeland Secure Data Network (HSDN) 20

IC Tradecraft Standards for Analysts Workshop 21

Managing Analysis Workshop 21

Mid-Level Intelligence and Threat Analysis Course 21

Open Source Practitioners Course (OSINT) 21

Principles of Intelligence Writing and Briefing 21

Regional Analytic Advisor Plan (RAAP) 22

State and Major Urban Area Fusion Centers 22

Vulnerabilities and Threat Risk Assessment (VTRA) Course 22

Immigration and Customs Enforcement (ICE) **23**

Office of State, Local and Tribal Coordination (OSLTC) 23

Blue Campaign to Combat Human Trafficking 23

If You Have the Right to Work, Don't Let Anyone Take it Away Poster 24

Law Enforcement Information Sharing Services (ICE Pattern Analysis and Information Collection
System) 24

Law Enforcement Support Center (LESC) 24

Resources for Victims of Human Trafficking and Other Crimes 25

Victim Assistance Program (VAP) 25

Homeland Security Investigations (HSI) Tipline Unit 25

Office of Infrastructure Protection (IP) **26**

Active Shooter Resources 26

Business Continuity Planning Suite 26

Critical Infrastructure and Key Resource (CIKR) Asset Protection Technical Assistance Program (CAPTAP) 26

Critical Infrastructure Toolkit 27

Dams Sector Crisis Management Handbook..27

Emergency Services Self-Assessment Tool (ESSAT) 27

Food and Agriculture Sector Criticality Assessment Tool (FASCAT) 28

Guide to Critical Infrastructure and Key Resources (CIKR) Protection at the State, Regional, Local, Tribal, & Territorial Level 28

Homeland Security Information Network-Critical Sectors (HSIN-CS) 28

Infrastructure Protection Program 28

Infrastructure Protection Sector-Specific Table Top Exercise Program (SSTEP) for the Commercial Facilities Retail/Lodging Subsectors and Sports Leagues/Public Assembly Subsectors 29

IS-906 Workplace Security Awareness...29

IS-907 - Active Shooter: What You Can Do 29

IS-921 Implementing Critical Infrastructure Protection Programs 30

Improvised Explosive Device (IED) Counterterrorism Workshop 30

Protective Measures Course 30

Surveillance Detection Course for Law Enforcement and Security Professionals 30

Improvised Explosive Device (IED) Awareness/Bomb Threat Management Workshop 31

Improvised Explosive Device (IED) Search Procedures Workshop 31

National Capabilities Analysis Database (NCAD) 31

Multi-Jurisdiction Improvised Explosive Device Security Planning (MJIEDSP) 31

Bomb-making Materials Awareness Program (BMAP) 31

Technical Resource for Incident Prevention (TRIPwire) 31

Protective Security Advisor (PSA) Program 32

Enhanced Critical Infrastructure Protection Program (ECIP) Security Survey 32

Regional Resiliency Assessment Program (RRAP) 33

Regional Resiliency Assessment Program (RRAP) Discussion Based Exercises 33

Risk Self-Assessment Tool for Stadiums and Arenas, Performing Art Centers, Lodging, Convention Centers, Racetracks, and Theme Parks...33

State and Local Implementation Snapshot 33

Suspicious Activity Reporting for Critical Infrastructure Tool..34

The Evolving Threat: What You Can Do 34

Webinar: The Ready Responder Program for the Emergency Services Sector.........................34

Office of Emergency Communications (OEC) **35**

SAFECOM Sector...35

Statewide Communication Interoperability Plans (SCIPs) 35

Interoperable Communications Technical Assistance Program (ICTAP) 35

The Government Emergency Telecommunications Service (GETS) 36

Wireless Priority Service (WPS) 36

Telecommunications Service Priority (TSP) 36

Regional Coordination Program 36

Southwest Border Communications Working Group (SWBCWG) 37

Office of Health Affairs (OHA) **38**

Guidance for Protecting Responders' Health During the First Week Following A Wide-Area Aerosol Anthrax Attack 38

National Biosurveillance Integration Center (NBIC) Strategic Plan 38

Planning for 2009 H1N1 Influenza: A Preparedness Guide for Small Business 38

Privacy Office **39**

DHS Privacy Policy Guidance 39

Privacy Impact Assessments (PIAs) 39

System of Records Notices (SORNs) 39

Privacy Office Reports to Congress 39

Freedom of Information Act (FOIA) 39

FOIA Reports 40

Science and Technology Directorate (S&T) **41**

FirstResponder.gov 41

First Responder Communities of Practice 41

Centers of Excellence (COE) 41

Transportation Security Administration (TSA) **42**

Airspace Waivers 42

Counterterrorism Guides 42

DVD-based training programs 43

First Observer Program 43

Freight Rail Security Awareness Brochure 43

General Aviation (GA) Secure Hotline 44

General Aviation Security Guidelines 44

Highway Government and Sector Coordinating Council 44

HMC Brochures 44

HMC I-Step Program 44

IED Recognition and Detection for Railroad Industry Employees Training CD 44

Law Enforcement Officers Flying Armed (LEOFA)/ National Law Enforcement Telecommunications
System (NLETS) Program 45

Recommended GA Security Action Items 45

TSA Pipeline Security Guidelines and Pipeline Smart Security Practice Observations 45

TSA Website/ Highway & Motor Carrier E-mail 45

TSA Security Clearance 46

United States Coast Guard (USCG) **47**

America's Waterways Watch 47

U.S. Coast Guard Maritime Information eXchange ("CGMIX") 47

U.S. Coast Guard Navigation Center 47

Additional Resources **48**

Department Wide Resources 48

Environmental Justice Program 48

Homeland Security Information Network (HSIN) 48

The DHS Veterans Employment Program Directive 3011 48

Office of Biometric Identity Management (OBIM) 49

DHS Grants 50

Assistance to Firefighter Grants (AFG) 50

Community Assistance Program, State Support Services Element (CAP-SSSE) 50

Community Disaster Loan Program 50

Emergency Management Performance Grant (EMPG) 50

Fire Management Assistance Grant Program 51

Fire Prevention and Safety Grants (FP&S) 51

Flood Mitigation Assistance Program 51

Hazard Mitigation Grant Program (HMGP) 51

Homeland Security Grant Program (HSGP) 51

Pre -Disaster Mitigation Program (PDM) 52

Public Assistance Grant Program (PA) 52

Reimbursement for Firefighting on Federal Property 52

Staffing For Adequate Fire & Emergency Response Grants (SAFER) 52

Tribal Homeland Security Grant Program (THSGP) 53

Private Sector and Community Engagement 54

FEMA Industry Liaison Program... 54

FEMA Small Business Industry Liaison Program 54

Office of Small and Disadvantaged Business Utilization (OSDBU).. 54

Research and Product Development 55

CBP Laboratories and Scientific Services 55

Defense Technology Experimental Research (DETER).. 55

DHS Small Business Innovation Research (SBIR) Program 55

DHS Technology Transfer Program 55

Homeland Open Security Technologies... 55

Mass Transit Security Technology Testing... 56

Minority Serving Institutions (MSIs) Programs 56

National Urban Security Technology Laboratory 56

Appendix A 57

Department of Homeland Security Contacts 57

U.S. Customs and Border Protection (CBP)

U.S. Customs and Border Protection (CBP) is one of the Department of Homeland Security's largest and most complex components, with a priority mission of keeping terrorists, criminals and their weapons out of the United States. CBP also has responsibility for securing and facilitating trade and travel while enforcing hundreds of U.S. regulations, including immigration and drug laws. For more information, visit www.cbp.gov.

CBP INFO Center Self Service Q&A Database

The CBP INFO Center Self Service Q&A Database is a searchable database with over 750 answers to commonly (and not so commonly) asked questions about CBP programs, requirements, and procedures. If visitors to the site are unable to find an answer to their question, they may submit an inquiry for personal assistance, an anonymous complaint, compliment, comment or one that requires a response. To use the searchable database, please visit https://help.cbp.gov/app/home, or call the CBP INFO Center at (877) CBP-5511 or (202) 325-8000.

National Gang Intelligence Center (NGIC)

The NGIC is a multi-agency effort that integrates the gang intelligence assets of federal, state, and local law enforcement entities to serve as a centralized intelligence resource for gang information and analytical support.

The mission of the NGIC is to support law enforcement agencies through timely and accurate information sharing and strategic/tactical analysis of federal, state, and local law enforcement intelligence focusing on the growth, migration, criminal activity, and association of gangs that pose a significant threat to communities throughout the United States.

The NGIC concentrates on gangs operating on a national level that demonstrate criminal connectivity between sets and common identifiers and goals. Because many violent gangs do not operate on a national level, the NGIC will also focus on regional-level gangs. The NGIC produces intelligence assessments, intelligence bulletins, joint agency intelligence products, and other non-standard intelligence products for our customers. For more information, please contact the NGIC, (703) 414-8600. Report any suspicious activity to 1-800-BE-ALERT.

CBP Border Community Liaison (BCL) Program

Border Community Liaisons focus on outreach to community stakeholders and provide fact-based information regarding the CBP mission, functions, authorities, and responsibilities.

BCLs nationwide can be accessed through the CBP State, Local, Tribal Liaison Office at 202-325-0775 or by emailing CBP-STATE-LOCAL-TRIBAL-LIAISON@cbp.dhs.gov.

CBP Information Center

The information center provides general information about CBP requirements and procedures, as well as handling the intake for complaints related to CBP interactions. The CBP INFO Center also maintains an on-line database of Q&A's covering all aspects of customs and immigration operations.

The CBP INFO Center can be reached at (877) CBP-5511 or 202-325-8000 or via the CBP.GOV website at https://help.cbp.gov/app/home.

CBP State, Local and Tribal Liaison (SLT)

As a component of the CBP Commissioner's Office, the State, Local and Tribal Liaison (SLT) strives to build and maintain effective relationships with state, local and tribal governments through regular, transparent and proactive communication.

Governmental questions regarding issues and policy pertaining to border security, trade, and facilitation can be referred to the SLT at 202-325-0775 or by emailing CBP-STATE-LOCAL-TRIBAL-LIAISON@cbp.dhs.gov.

CBP Tip Line

Suspicious activity regarding international travel and trade can be reported to CBP at 1-800-BE-ALERT.

Office for Civil Rights and Civil Liberties (CRCL)

The Department of Homeland Security **Office for Civil Rights and Civil Liberties (CRCL)** supports the Department's mission to secure the nation while preserving individual liberty, fairness, and equality under the law. CRCL integrates civil rights and civil liberties into all of the Department activities by:

- Promoting respect for civil rights and civil liberties in policy creation and implementation by advising Department leadership and personnel, and state and local partners.
- Communicating with individuals and communities whose civil rights and civil liberties may be affected by Department activities, informing them about policies and avenues of redress, and promoting appropriate attention within the Department to their experiences and concerns.
- Investigating and resolving civil rights and civil liberties complaints filed by the public regarding Department policies or activities, or actions taken by Department personnel.
- Leading the Department's equal employment opportunity programs and promoting workforce diversity and merit system principles.

For more information on CRCL, visit the website at http://www.dhs.gov/office-civil-rights-and-civil-liberties.

Civil Rights Requirements in Federally Assisted Programs

CRCL provides resources, guidance, and technical assistance to recipients of DHS financial assistance on complying with Title VI of the Civil Rights Act of 1964 (Title VI), Section 504 of the Rehabilitation Act of 1973, and related statutes. Information for recipients on meeting their nondiscrimination requirements under Title VI is available on CRCL's website, http://www.dhs.gov/title-vi-overview-recipients-dhs-financial-assistance. For more information on Section 504 of the Rehabilitation Act of 1973, visit http://www.dol.gov/oasam/regs/statutes/sec504.htm.

CRCL also provides guidance to help those who carry out Department-supported activities to understand and implement their obligations under Title VI to provide meaningful access for people with limited English proficiency (LEP). For more information, visit http://www.dhs.gov/guidance-published-help-department-supported-organizations-provide-meaningful-access-people-limited, or contact crcl@dhs.gov.

Community Roundtables

CRCL leads or plays a significant role in regular roundtable meetings across the country in more than 14 cities. These roundtables bring together diverse communities with government representatives to discuss civil rights and civil liberties concerns ranging from immigration and border issues to travel and aviation security. CRCL also conducts roundtables with young leaders of diverse communities. For more information please contact Community Engagement@dhs.gov.

CRCL Impact Assessments

CRCL uses impact assessments to review Department programs, policies, and activities to determine whether these initiatives have an impact on the civil rights and civil liberties of those affected by the initiative. For more information about CRCL Impact Assessments, please visit http://www.dhs.gov/civil-rights-civil-liberties-impact-assessments.

CRCL Newsletter

CRCL distributes a monthly newsletter to inform its stakeholders and the public about CRCL news and activities, including ongoing and upcoming projects; how to file complaints; and opportunities to offer comments and feedback.

Newsletters are distributed via an email list to thousands of NGOs, community members, and government partners, and made available to community groups for redistribution. For more information, visit http://www.dhs.gov/office-civil-rights-and-civil-liberties-newsletter, or contact CRCLOutreach@dhs.gov.

CRCL Facebook Page

CRCL created a Facebook page to enhance its regular contact with community stakeholders. This outreach tool allows the office to inform a wider audience about the CRCL mission, incorporating civil rights and civil liberties protections into all DHS programs and activities. For more information, visit http://www.facebook.com/CivilRightsAndCivilLiberties.

Equal Employment Opportunity (EEO) Reports

CRCL's EEO and Diversity Division prepares and submits a variety of reports relating to the Department's EEO activities. For more information, visit http://www.dhs.gov/eeo-and-diversity-reports-and-resources.

E-Verify and Unfair Labor Practices Training

CRCL provides training on worker rights and the responsibilities imposed upon the private sector when using E-Verify and verifying employment eligibility. Training includes best practices, examples of unlawful practices against workers, remedies for workers, and instructions for how to prepare a human resources department. The training assists employer understanding of how to use E-Verify in a responsible manner without violating prohibitions against discrimination.

In collaboration with U.S. Citizenship and Immigration Services, CRCL has created two videos, *Understanding E-Verify: Employer Responsibilities and Worker Rights* and *Know Your Rights: Employee Rights and Responsibilities*, to ensure employers and employees are knowledgeable about their rights and responsibilities. To view the videos, please visit www.dhs.gov/E-Verify or www.youtube.com/ushomelandsecurity. For more information, contact CRCL at crcltraining@dhs.gov, or call 1-866-644-8360.

Forced Labor Resources

The ICE Office of International Affairs investigates allegations of forced labor in violation of the Tariff Act of 1930 (19 U.S.C. § 1307). To request more information or a copy of the *A Forced Child Labor Advisory* booklet and brochure, please contact labor.iceforced@dhs.gov.

If contacting ICE to report instances of imported goods mined, produced, or manufactured by forced labor, please provide as much detailed information and supporting documentation as possible, including the following: a full statement of the reasons for the belief that the product was produced by forced labor and that it may be or has been imported into the United States; a detailed description of the product; and all pertinent facts known regarding the production of the product abroad.

For the location of ICE foreign offices, please visit the ICE web site at http://www.ice.gov, click About Us, click International Affairs and select your country. ICE maintains a 24/7 hotline at (866) DHS-2-ICE.

How to File and Submit a Complaint

Under 6 U.S.C. § 345 and 42 U.S.C. § 2000ee-1, CRCL reviews and assesses information concerning abuses of civil rights, civil liberties, and profiling on the basis of race, ethnicity, or religion, by employees and officials of the Department of Homeland Security. Complaints are accepted in languages other than English. For more information visit: www.dhs.gov/crcl.

Human Rights and Vulnerable Populations

CRCL is the DHS single point of contact for international human rights treaty reporting and coordination. In coordinating treaty reporting for the Department, CRCL works across DHS and with other federal agencies and departments. At DHS, CRCL also ensures that U.S. human rights obligations are considered in Department policies and programs. For more information please contact HumanRightsOfficer@dhs.gov.

Human Rights Violators and War Crimes Unit

The Human Rights Violators and War Crimes Unit protects the public by targeting war criminals and those who violate human rights, including violators living both domestically and abroad. ICE investigators, intelligence analysts, and attorneys work with governmental and non-governmental agencies to accept tips and information from those who report suspected war criminals and human rights violators. Individuals seeking to report these abuses of human rights may contact the center at HRV.ICE@DHS.GOV.

Privacy, Civil Rights and Civil Liberties Fusion Center Training Program

The Implementing Recommendations of the 9/11 Commission Act requires that DHS support Fusion Centers in training on privacy, civil rights, and civil liberties. As a result, CRCL and the DHS Privacy Office have partnered with the DHS Office of Intelligence & Analysis State and Local Program Office and the DOJ Bureau of Justice Assistance to deliver this training program.

The program has four elements: a website Resource center found at www.it.ojp.gov/PrivacyLiberty, a training of Privacy/Civil Liberties Officers program, technical assistance, and an on-site training program. Topics covered include: civil rights and civil liberties basics and red flags (how to spot potential issues and incorporate safeguards into your procedures); privacy fundamentals (how to integrate your privacy policy and recognize and respond to a privacy incident); cultural tactics for intelligence and law enforcement professionals (covers frequently encountered misconceptions and stereotypes and addresses policies against racial or ethnic profiling); and First Amendment issues in the information sharing environment (covers considerations when fusion centers may encounter constitutionally protected activities, such as freedom of speech, demonstrations, petitions for redress, etc.).

Fusion Centers and their liaison officer networks have the option of choosing additional topics to create a customized agenda. Technical assistance is also available. Duration: full-day (8 hours) but can be customized to shorter sessions. For more information, contact FusionCenterTraining@dhs.gov.

Quarterly NGO Civil Rights / Civil Liberties Committee Meetings
CRCL hosts regular meetings with representatives of over 20 civil society organizations primarily working on matters at the intersection of immigration and civil and human rights. Assisted by extensive grassroots networks, committee members articulate the concerns of organizations and communities across the country on these issues. The CRCL Officer meets quarterly with the Committee to identify systemic and policy concerns relevant to CRCL. For more information, contact CRCLOutreach@dhs.gov.

Office for Civil Rights and Civil Liberties (CRCL) Quarterly and Annual Reports to Congress
Under 6 U.S.C. § 345 and 42 U.S.C. § 2000ee-1, CRCL is required to report quarterly and annually to Congress about the activities of the Office. For more information, or to view the reports, visit www.dhs.gov/reports-office-civil-rights-and-civil-liberties.

Office of Cybersecurity and Communications (CS&C)

The **Office of Cybersecurity and Communications (CS&C)** is responsible for enhancing the security, resiliency, and reliability of the Nation's cyber and communications infrastructure. CS&C actively engages the public and private sectors as well as international partners to prepare for, prevent, and respond to catastrophic incidents that could degrade or overwhelm strategic assets.

CS&C works to prevent or minimize disruptions to our critical information infrastructure in order to protect the public, the economy, government services, and the overall security of the United States. It does this by supporting a series of continuous efforts designed to further safeguard federal government systems by reducing potential vulnerabilities, protecting against cyber intrusions, and anticipating future threats.

Within CS&C's Stakeholder Engagement and Cyber Infrastructure Resilience (SE/CIR) Division, the State, Local, Tribal, and Territorial (SLTT) Cybersecurity Engagement Program fosters the relationships that protect our Nation's critical infrastructure. Governors and other appointed and elected SLTT government officials receive cybersecurity risk briefings and information on available resources. More importantly, these officials look to the program to identify cybersecurity initiatives and partnership opportunities with federal agencies, as well as state and local associations, that will help protect their citizens online.

Partnership Opportunities:

Multi-State Information Sharing and Analysis Center (MS-ISAC)
The MS-ISAC, in partnership with DHS and the SLTT Cybersecurity Engagement Program, provides cybersecurity support and services to SLTT governments. Currently, DHS grant funding to the MS-ISAC provides cybersecurity services for the networks and systems of 22 states, seven local governments and one territory. For more information, contact the SLTT program at CSC_SLTT@hq.dhs.gov.

Critical Infrastructure Partnership Advisory Council (CIPAC)
The CIPAC is a Federal Advisory Committee Act (FACA)-exempt advisory committee established in 2008, at the direction of the Secretary of the Department of Homeland Security. The CIPAC is a forum composed of a wide cross-section of government and private sector participants including critical infrastructure owners and operators. The CIPAC is authorized to provide direct advice to Federal employees on a broad spectrum of critical infrastructure protection activities, like those addressed by the Cross-Sector Cyber Security Working Group. To learn more, email cipac@dhs.gov.

Information Technology-Government Coordinating Council (IT-GCC)
The IT-GCC brings together diverse federal, state, local and tribal interests to identify and develop collaborative strategies that advance IT critical infrastructure protection. The IT-GCC serves as a counterpart to the IT-Sector Coordinating Council (IT-SCC).

Cyber Assessments, Evaluations, and Reviews:

Cyber Security Evaluation Tool (CSET)

The CSET provides a systematic and repeatable approach to assess the cybersecurity posture of Industrial Control System (ICS) networks. CSET is a stand-alone software tool that enables users to assess their network and ICS security practices against industry and government standards and it provides prioritized recommendations. To request a CSET CD, email cset@dhs.gov. For all other questions, email cssp@dhs.gov or visit www.us-cert.gov/control_systems/.

Cybersecurity Assessment and Risk Management Approach (CARMA)

CARMA assists public and private sector partners assess, prioritize, and manage cyber infrastructure risk by providing a picture of sector-wide risks for different categories of cyber critical infrastructure. For more information, email NCSD_CIP-CS@dhs.gov.

Software Assurance Assistance:

Software Assurance Forum

The Software Assurance Forum brings public and private stakeholders together to discuss ways to advance software assurance objectives. Through collaborative events, stakeholders raise expectations for product assurance with requisite levels of integrity and security, and promote security methodologies and tools as a normal part of business.

"Build Security In" (BSI)

BSI is a collaborative effort to provide tools, guidelines, and other resources that software developers, architects, and security practitioners can use to build security into software in every phase of development. For more information, visit https://buildsecurityin.us-cert.gov/swa or email software.assurance@dhs.gov.

Exercises and Training:

CyberStorm Exercise Series

The CyberStorm Exercise Series focuses on simulated cyber-specific threat scenarios intended to highlight critical infrastructure interdependence and further integrate federal, state, international, and private sector response and recovery efforts. The series helps participants assess their response and coordination capabilities specific to a cyber incident. Contact CEP@dhs.gov for more information.

Operations Centers and Emergency Response and Readiness Teams:

National Cybersecurity Communications Integration Center (NCCIC)

The NCCIC provides 24-hour support for cyber and communications incidents and includes the United States Computer Emergency Readiness Team (US-CERT), the Industrial Control Systems Cyber Emergency Response Team (ICS-CERT), and the National Coordinating Center for Telecommunications (NCC), along with representatives from the DHS Office of Intelligence and Analysis, law enforcement, the intelligence community, the Department of Defense, state and local governments, and the private sector.

It is the lead Federal operations center for the protection of federal civilian agencies in cyberspace, providing support and expertise to critical infrastructure owners and operators, working through the Multi State Information Sharing and Analysis Center (MS-ISAC) to provide expertise and information to State and Local governments, plus coordination with international partners to share information and collaboratively respond to incidents.

United States Computer Emergency Readiness Team (US-CERT)

US-CERT, part of the National Cybersecurity Communications Integration Center (NCCIC), works to improve the Nation's cybersecurity posture by identifying and analyzing suspicious activity, probable intrusions, and confirmed events, as well as responding appropriately to manage risk. US-CERT receives data from multiple sources including federal agencies; state, local, tribal and territorial (SLTT) governments; the private sector; and international partners. It uses that information to provide comprehensive analysis, mitigation strategies, and timely and actionable alert and warning information with its partners and constituents. US-CERT maintains robust intrusion detection, incident analysis, warning, and response capabilities. Upon request, US-CERT provides on-site incident response capabilities to Federal and State agencies. To report suspicious cyber activity, call US-CERT at (888) 828-0870 or email soc@us-cert.gov.

National Cyber Alert System (NCAS)

US-CERT's National Cyber Alert System delivers timely and actionable information and threat products, including alerts, bulletins and tips to users of all technical levels. Visit www.us-cert.gov/cas/signup.html to subscribe.

Industrial Control Systems Cyber Emergency Response Team (ICS-CERT)

ICS-CERT coordinates control systems-related security incidents and information sharing through use of **Fly-Away Teams** with federal, state, and local agencies and organizations, the intelligence community, the private sector constituents, and international and private sector CERTs.

ICS-CERT also operates a **Malware Lab** to analyze vulnerabilities and malware threats to ICS equipment. To report suspicious cyber activity affecting ICS, call the ICS-CERT Watch Floor at (877) 776-7585 or email ics-cert@dhs.gov.

Outreach and Awareness:

National Cyber Security Awareness Month and Stop.Think.Connect Campaign

CS&C's SE/CIR Division collaborates with its partners, including the National Cyber Security Alliance (NCSA) and the MS-ISAC, to support public outreach and awareness activities, including National Cyber Security Awareness Month and the Stop.Think.Connect. Campaign. The SLTT Cybersecurity Engagement Program has been essential to the continued success of this annual event, helping to secure resolutions from all 50 states. In partnership with MS-ISAC and CS&C's External Affairs, the SLTT Cybersecurity Engagement Program works to sponsor events and activities throughout the country and disseminate Awareness Month key messages to state and local partners. To learn more or to book a speaker for an upcoming event, visit www.dhs.gov/cyber or www.dhs.gov/stopthinkconnect.

Government Forum of Incident Response and Security (GFIRST)
GFIRST is a Government information-sharing effort focused on daily information exchange among technical operators across the defense, intelligence, law enforcement, and federal civilian agency communities. The annual GFIRST National Conference gathers partners and analysts to share advances in incident response and best practices to strengthen cybersecurity. For more information, visit www.us-cert.gov/gfirst.

Domestic Nuclear Detection Office (DNDO)

The Domestic Nuclear Detection Office (DNDO) is a jointly staffed office within the Department of Homeland Security. DNDO is the primary entity in the U.S. government for implementing domestic nuclear detection efforts for a managed and coordinated response to radiological and nuclear threats, as well as integration of federal nuclear forensics programs. Additionally, DNDO is charged with coordinating the development of the global nuclear detection and reporting architecture, with partners from federal, state, local, and international governments and the private sector. For more information, see http://www.dhs.gov/about-domestic-nuclear-detection-office or contact DNDO.INFO@hq.dhs.gov.

Radiological /Nuclear Detection and Adjudication Capability Development Framework (CDF)

The CDF planning guidance assists state, local, and tribal jurisdictions with identifying and developing recommended levels of radiological and nuclear (rad/nuc) detection capability based on risk factors and the likelihood of encountering illicit rad/nuc material. The CDF is based on lessons learned provided by federal, state, and local subject matter experts. It is intended to provide strategic guidance based on best practices, but not to establish specific requirements. The CDF is a DNDO product modeled on the FEMA Target Capability List (TCL) version 3.0, and can be leveraged to support investment justifications. A CDF Calculator is also available to assist jurisdictions with identifying recommended levels of rad/nuc detection capability quickly and easily. The CDF and supporting resources are available on the PRND Community of Interest (COI) web portal (see below) or by contacting DNDO at DNDO.SLA@hq.dhs.gov.

National Incident Management System (NIMS) Preventive Radioactive/Nuclear Detection Resource (PRND) Type Definitions

The NIMS Resource Type Definitions were developed in 2011 with direct state and local participation to assist state, local, and tribal stakeholders with defining and building rad/nuc detection capability and to allow jurisdictions the ability to categorize and deploy resources through the Emergency Management Assistance Compact (EMAC) or other interstate mutual aid agreements and compacts. The PRND Resource Types categorize equipment, teams, and personnel consistent with other NIMS resource types to facilitate identification, inventory, and tracking. The PRND NIMS Resource Type Definitions and supporting resources can be obtained on the PRND Community of Interest (COI) web portal (see below), by contacting DNDO at DNDO.SLA@hq.dhs.gov or in the DNDO FY2012 HSGP Supplemental Resource at http://www.fema.gov/sites/default/files/orig/fema_pdfs/pdf/government/grant/2012/fy12_hsgp_dndo.pdf.

Training

DNDO training provides quality products and support to develop, enhance, and expand radiological and nuclear detection capabilities in support of the Global Nuclear Detection Architecture (GNDA). Together with federal partners, the DNDO training program provides technical review, evaluation, and continual developmental improvement of the radiological and nuclear detection training curriculum to increase the operational detection capabilities of federal, state, local and tribal agencies to detect and interdict radiological and nuclear materials and/or devices. The program seeks to develop and exercise protocols and training standards for effective use of radiation detection equipment and the associated alarm reporting and resolution processes and to develop training curricula in support of emerging detection technologies and operational profiles. DNDO and its partners have completed radiological and nuclear detection training for over 23,000 law enforcement, first responder personnel and public officials through FY12.

Nuclear detection training courses are available through FEMA's National Preparedness Directorate. Courses are taught by the National Domestic Preparedness Consortium member – Counter Terrorism Operations Support (CTOS) training organization. The CTOS Web page can be found at http://www.ctosnnsa.org/. Courses are also available through the FEMA Federal Sponsored Course catalog.

For more information on FEMA FSCC, visit their website located at https://www.firstrespondertraining.gov/webforms/pdfs/fed_catalog.pdf. DNDO can be contacted to discuss PRND training program questions, course needs, or special requests by emailing DNDOTRAINING@hq.dhs.gov.

Exercises

DNDO provides assistance in developing, designing, and conducting exercises that are compliant with the Homeland Security Exercise and Evaluation Program (HSEEP) methodology. The exercises provide valuable hands-on experience for personnel performing radiation detection missions and assist decision makers in integrating the PRND mission into their daily operations. Additional information about PRND exercises is available by contacting DNDO at DNDO.SLA@hq.dhs.gov.

Joint Analysis Center (JAC)

The Joint Analysis Center provides awareness of the GNDA and provides technical support to federal, state, local and tribal authorities. Utilizing the Joint Analysis Center Collaborative Information System (JACCIS), the JAC facilitates nuclear and radiological alarm adjudication from detection events and consolidates and shares information and databases.

JACCIS provides a process for federal, state, tribal, territorial and local agencies to share radiological and nuclear detection information at the Unclassified/Official Use Only level.

The JAC provides information integration and analysis coupled with awareness of the GNDA. This enables the right information to be available at the point of detection and ensures that detection events result in either a proper response to a threat or a quick dismissal of a non-threat. To contact the JAC, call 866-789-8304, or e-mail DNDO.JAC2@hq.dhs.gov. For more information, visit http://www.dhs.gov/xabout/structure/editorial_0766.shtm.

Federal Emergency Management Agency (FEMA)

The **Federal Emergency Management Agency's (FEMA)** mission is to support our citizens and first responders to ensure that as a Nation we work together to build, sustain, and improve our capability to prepare for, protect against, respond to, recover from, and mitigate all hazards. For more information, visit www.fema.gov.

Community Emergency Response Team (CERT)

CERT helps to train people to be better prepared to respond to emergency situations in their communities. It is a resource available to support both the public and private sectors to use to ensure its employees are prepared for all hazards. During emergencies, CERT members can give critical support to first responders, provide immediate assistance to survivors, and organize volunteers at a disaster site. CERT members can also help with non-emergency projects that help improve the safety of the community. For more information, visit www.citizencorps.gov/cert or contact cert@dhs.gov.

DisasterAssistance.gov

DisasterAssistance.gov is a secure, user-friendly U.S. government web portal that consolidates disaster assistance information in one place. If you need assistance following a presidentially declared disaster that has been designated for individual assistance, go to http://www.DisasterAssistance.gov to register online. Local resource information to help keep citizens safe during an emergency is also available. Currently, 17 U.S. government agencies, which sponsor almost 60 forms of assistance, contribute to the portal. For web site technical assistance, contact (800) 745-0243.

Emergency Management Institute Programs (EMI)

The Emergency Management Institute offers numerous programs that are designed for people who have emergency management responsibilities. The training is free of charge; however, individuals from the private sector or contractors to State, local or Tribal governments must pay their own transportation and lodging fees.

EMI has an integrated training approach and encourages individuals from private sector to participate in our courses. EMI's programs include, but are not limited to, the Master Trainer Program, Master Exercise Practitioner Program, Professional Development Series, Applied Practices Series and FEMA's Higher Education Program. For more information, see http://www.training.fema.gov/Programs/ or call (301) 447-1286.

Flood Map Assistance Center (FMAC)

The Flood Map Assistance Center provides information to the public about National Flood Insurance Program rules, regulations, and procedures. The FMAC is often the first point of contact between FEMA and various flood map users.

The FMAC's goal is to provide the appropriate information to callers to help them understand the technical issues involved in a particular situation. In addition to taking incoming telephone calls, Map

Specialists respond to mapping-related e-mail inquiries, and also review and process Letter of Map Amendment (LOMA), Letter of Map Revision Based on Fill (LOMR-F), and Letter of Determination Review (LODR) requests. There are available resources for Engineers/Surveyors, Insurance Professionals and Lenders, and Floodplain Managers. For more information, call (877) FEMA-MAP (877-336-2627) or e-mail FEMAMapSpecialist@riskmapcds.com.

Private Sector E-alert

The FEMA Private Sector Division, Office of External Affairs, publishes periodic e-alerts providing timely information on topics of interest to private sector entities. The FEMA Private Sector Web Portal aggregates FEMA's online resources for the private sector. Content includes best practices in public-private partnerships, weekly preparedness tips, links to training opportunities, planning and preparedness resources, information on how to do business with FEMA, and more. For more information, visit www.fema.gov/privatesector. Sign up for the alert at FEMA-Private-Sector-Web@dhs.gov.

Incident Command System (ICS)

The ICS is a standardized, on-scene, all-hazards incident management approach that allows for the integration of facilities, equipment, personnel, procedures, and communications operating within a common organizational structure; enables a coordinated response among various jurisdictions and functional agencies, both public and private; and establishes common processes for planning and managing resources.

ICS is flexible and can be used for incidents of any type, scope, and complexity. ICS allows its users to adopt an integrated organizational structure to match the complexities and demands of single or multiple incidents.

ICS is used by all levels of government—federal, state, tribal, and local—as well as by many nongovernmental organizations and the private sector. ICS is also applicable across disciplines. It is typically structured to facilitate activities in five major functional areas: Command, Operations, Planning, Logistics, and Finance/Administration. All of the functional areas may or may not be used based on the incident needs. Intelligence/Investigations is an optional sixth functional area that is activated on a case-by-case basis.

As a system, ICS is extremely useful; not only does it provide an organizational structure for incident management, but it also guides the process for planning, building, and adapting that structure. Using ICS for every incident or planned event helps hone and maintain skills needed for the large-scale incidents.

Map Modernization Management Support (MMMS)

The FEMA Federal Insurance and Mitigation Administration (FIMA) distributes a guidance document each year to assist FEMA staff and Cooperating Technical Partners (CTP) in preparing, developing, and managing CTP activities. This document addresses administration, funded activities, eligibility and evaluation criteria, reporting requirements, technical capabilities, contracting requirements, standards, certification, funding, and cooperative agreement management for the CTP Program.

For more information on FIMA, visit http://www.fema.gov/what-mitigation/federal-insurance-mitigation-administration. To read the guidance document, visit http://www.fema.gov/library/viewRecord.do?id=2924.

National Flood Insurance Program (NFIP)

The National Flood Insurance Program focuses on Flood Insurance, Floodplain Management, and Flood Hazard Mapping. Nearly 20,000 communities across the U.S. and its territories participate in the NFIP by adopting and enforcing floodplain management ordinances to reduce future flood damage. In exchange, the NFIP makes federally-backed flood insurance available to homeowners, renters, and business owners in these communities. See www.floodsmart.gov for more information. Flood insurance agents should visit www.agents.floodsmart.gov or e-mail asktheexpert@riskmapcds.com.

National Incident Management System (NIMS)

The National Incident Management System provides a systematic, proactive approach to guide the public and private sector in coordinating and managing the response to all hazards. NIMS is a scalable system based upon organization and common terminology that assist departments and agencies at all levels of government, nongovernmental organizations, and the private sector to work seamlessly to prevent, protect against, respond to, recover from, and mitigate the effects of incidents, regardless of cause, size, location, or complexity, in order to reduce the loss of life and property and harm to the environment. For more information, visit www.fema.gov/nims. Questions regarding NIMS should be directed to FEMA-NIMS@dhs.gov or (202) 646-3850.

National Response Framework (NRF)

The National Response Framework is a set of guiding principles for how the Nation prevents, protects against, responds to, recovers from, and mitigates the effects of incidents presents the guiding principles that enable all response partners to prepare for and provide a unified national response to disasters and emergencies—from the smallest incident to the largest catastrophe. The *Framework* establishes a comprehensive, national, all-hazards approach to domestic incident response. For more information, visit http://www.fema.gov/nrf.

National Training and Education Division (NTED)

National Training and Education Division (NTED) courses are delivered in the following formats:
- Resident – Instructor-led classroom training is provided at a training facility.
- Mobile – Also referred to as non-resident, mobile training can be performed by FEMA funded instructors at any location.
- Web-Based – Web-based or 'online' training is done via the internet and is often self-paced (no instructor).
- Indirect – Indirect training includes training courses taught by instructors (non-FEMA or training partner staff) that have completed a 'Train the Trainer' course.

For more information, visit www.training.fema.gov. Contact the program via phone at (800) 368-6498 or e-mail askCSID@dhs.gov.

Ready Indian Country

FEMA, as part of the federal government, has a nation-to-nation relationship with Alaska Native and Tribal governments as reflected in our Tribal Policy. FEMA works with Tribal officials to help communities be prepared before an emergency and recover afterward. Readiness planning is essential for all American Indians and Alaska Natives, and there are special considerations when families live on tribal lands located far from urban centers.

For ordering publications on Ready, contact FEMA-Publications-Warehouse@FEMA.gov or call 1-800-BE-READY (1-800-237-3239). Multiple copies can also be requested by downloading the Ready Publications Order Form (PDF) at http://www.ready.gov/sites/default/files/Ready_OrderForm_June2012.pdf, and mailing or faxing it to the FEMA Warehouse. For more information, visit http://www.ready.gov/make-a-plan/indian-country.

Emergency Lodging Assistance Program

The Emergency Lodging Assistance Program provides prompt lodging payments for short term stays in the event of a declared disaster. The program is administered by Corporate Lodging Consultants, a federal government contractor and the largest outsourced lodging services provider in North America.

For more information, see http://ela.corplodging.com/programinfo.php , contact femahousing@corplodging.com , or call (866) 545-9865.

Voluntary Private Sector Preparedness Accreditation and Certification Program (PS-Prep)

The purpose of PS-Prep is to enhance nationwide resilience in an all-hazards environment by encouraging private sector preparedness. The program provides a mechanism by which a private sector entity such as a company, facility, not-for-profit corporation, hospital, stadium, or university, can certify that it conforms to one or more preparedness standards adopted by DHS. Participation in the PS-Prep program is completely voluntary.

No private sector entity will be required by DHS to comply with any standard adopted under the program. However, DHS encourages all private sector entities to seriously consider seeking certification on one or more standards that will be adopted by DHS.

Tornado Safety Initiative

The Tornado Safety Initiative assesses building damages and identifies lessons learned after tornadoes occur; funds research on shelter design and construction standards; develops best practices and technical manuals on safe rooms and community shelters; and produces public education materials on tornado preparedness and response. FEMA produces technical manuals for engineers, architects, building officials, and prospective shelter owners on the design and construction of safe rooms and community shelters. For more information, visit http://www.fema.gov/plan/prevent/saferoom/index.

U.S. Fire Administration's National Fire Academy (NFA) Training Programs

National Fire Academy Training Programs enhance the ability of fire and emergency services and allied professionals to deal more effectively with fire and related emergencies. NFA offers courses in the following subject areas: Arson Mitigation, Emergency Medical Services, Executive Development, Fire Prevention: Management, Fire Prevention: Public Education, Fire Prevention: Technical, Hazardous Materials, Incident Management, Management Science, Planning and Information Management and Training Programs. NFA offers residential training at its Emmitsburg, Maryland facility and off-campus training throughout the United States, as well as online self-study courses free of charge. For more information, see http://www.usfa.dhs.gov/nfa/index.shtm or call (301) 447-1000.

U.S. Fire Administration Publications

U.S. Fire Administration Publications encourage Americans, including private sector constituents, to practice fire safety and to protect themselves and their families from the dangers of fire. Order USFA publications online at http://www.usfa.dhs.gov/applications/publications/ Contact the U.S Fire Administration via email, usfa-publications@dhs.gov, or phone, (800)561-3356.

National Continuity Programs (NCP)

NCP provides Continuity of Operations (COOP) planning guidance, training, exercises, and assessments in developing capabilities for continuance of the federal government's essential functions, and providing integrated continuity guidance for all State, Territorial, Tribal and Local (STTL) governments across a broad spectrum of emergencies.

The Continuity of Operations program has developed a Tribal Continuity Video *"Introduction to Continuity of Operations for Tribal Governments",* EMI/Tribal Curriculum *"Continuity of Operations (COOP) for Tribal Governments L-552 Workshop",* Continuity Guidance Circular 1 (CGC 1), Continuity Guidance Circular 2 (CGC 2), and Continuity Assistance Tool (CAT). These Continuity products give Tribal governments a foundation for ensuring operation of essential government functions during emergency events. For more information, visit http://www.fema.gov/continuity-operations.

Questions regarding Tribal Continuity of Operations should be directed to FEMA-STTLContinuity@fema.dhs.gov. Tribes can register for National Continuity of Operations E-mail alerts at https://public.govdelivery.com/accounts/USDHSFEMA/subscriber/new?topic_id=USDHSFEMA_1010.

Federal Law Enforcement Training Centers (FLETC)

The **Federal Law Enforcement Training Centers (FLETC)** serves as an interagency, accredited law enforcement training organization that provides consolidated law enforcement training for 91 federal agencies. The FLETC also provides services to state, local, rural, tribal, territorial, and international law enforcement agencies. The FLETC is headquartered at Glynco, GA, near the port city of Brunswick, halfway between Savannah, GA, and Jacksonville, FL. In addition to Glynco, the FLETC operates two other residential training sites in Artesia, NM, and Charleston, SC. The FLETC also operates a non-residential in-service re-qualification and advanced training facility in Cheltenham, MD, for use by agencies with large concentrations of personnel in the Washington, D.C. area.

The FLETC has oversight and program management responsibilities at the International Law Enforcement Academies (ILEA) in Gaborone, Botswana, and Bangkok, Thailand. The FLETC also supports training at other ILEAs in Hungary and El Salvador.

Leadership and International Capacity Building Division / Leadership Institute Branch

The Leadership and International Capacity Building Division / Leadership Institute Branch at the FLETC delivers its training programs "seminar style" in facilities that are dedicated to and fashioned for law enforcement leaders. Classes are conducted in a conference facility that includes two classrooms, six breakout rooms, a relaxing lounge area and a business center complete with internet access, printers, copiers and facsimile services.

Our staff is committed to providing students not only with training that meets their leadership needs, but also with the support and service that recognizes and respects their leadership role. State, local, rural, tribal and territorial agencies are welcome to register.

Contact Information
Leadership Institute Branch
Leadership and International Capacity Building Division
Federal Law Enforcement Training Centers
1131 Chapel Crossing Road
Building 397
Glynco, GA 31524
Telephone: (912) 267-2153
Fax: (912) 267-2745
Email: FLETC-LeadershipInstituteBranch@fletc.dhs.gov

Office of State, Local, Rural, Tribal and Territorial Training (SLRTT)

The SLRTT at the FLETC provides tuition-free and low cost training to state, local, rural, tribal and territorial law enforcement agencies throughout the United States. These law enforcement training programs and courses of instruction are conducted across the country and are typically hosted by a Peace Officer Standards and Training (POST) Academy, or by a state, local, rural, tribal or territorial law enforcement agency and are based on their advanced training needs.

Additionally, this low cost or tuition-free law enforcement training is often offered at one of the FLETC's four training delivery points located in Glynco (Brunswick), GA; Artesia, NM; Charleston, SC; and Cheltenham, MD. The FLETC also conducts the Rural Police Officers Training Program for the Bureau of Indian Affairs to meet their basic law enforcement training needs.

The introductory and advanced training programs that the SLRTT delivers are developed with the advice, assistance and support of federal, state, local, rural, tribal, and territorial law enforcement agencies. Training is continuously updated to ensure accuracy and relevance to today's issues.

Contact Information
Office of State, Local, Rural, Tribal and Territorial Training

Federal Law Enforcement Training Centers
1131 Chapel Crossing Rd., Bldg. 2200
Glynco, GA 31524
Email: stateandlocaltraining@dhs.gov
Phone: (800) 743-5382 (912) 267-2345

Office of Intelligence and Analysis (I&A)

I&A's Intelligence Training Branch (ITB) designs, develops, assesses, and delivers intelligence training through a diverse set of training, education, and professional development programs for the Department of Homeland Security's (DHS) Intelligence Enterprise (IE) workforce and its federal, state, local, tribal, and territorial (SLTT), and private sector (PS) partners throughout the United States. I&A's tradecraft workshops provide specific guidance and practice in applying Intelligence Community (IC) analytic standards for improving the quality of intelligence products, as well as critical thinking and presentation skills. DHS Training Sponsorships are available to Tribal officials with an interest in homeland security. To obtain the latest I&A training catalog, contact IA-Registrar@hq.dhs.gov or call (202) 282-8866. For information about the analytic tradecraft workshops, contact IA_TradecraftWorkshops@hq.dhs.gov.

Alternative Analysis Workshop
This analytic tradecraft workshop focuses on several simple techniques that explore alternative explanations or hypotheses to help analysts avoid mindsets or frames of reference about a problem that can blind them to other possibilities.

Basic Intelligence and Threat Analysis Course
This ITB in-resident course provides students with the foundational knowledge of DHS analytical missions, processes, and procedures. The course modules include *Critical Thinking and Analytic Methods*; *Principles of Intelligence Writing and Briefing*; and *Vulnerability, Threat, and Risk Assessment*. Throughout the course, students apply their newly acquired knowledge in numerous homeland security practical exercises. Student knowledge is assessed through graded written products, briefings, quizzes, and examinations.

Clearance Nominations
Clearance nominations are available to tribal officials with a bona fide need to access classified information in the course of their official duties. These Tribal officials must be engaged with their fusion center and be committed to information sharing. To request clearance information contact the DHS representative at the fusion center located in the Tribe's state.

Critical Thinking and Analytic Methods Course
This entry level mobile training and distance learning course, provided by ITB for DHS analysts, provides foundational knowledge in critical thinking and analytic methodologies. Throughout the course, students apply critical thinking knowledge and analytical methodologies via a homeland security-based exercise. Student knowledge is assessed through written products and briefings.

Homeland Secure Data Network (HSDN)
HSDN is a classified, wide-area network that allows the federal government to move information and intelligence to state, local, tribal, and territorial (SLTT) partners at the Secret level. To obtain access to HSDN, a Tribal representative must be engaged with their fusion center that has a DHS Intelligence Officer embedded and have a Secret level clearance. For additional information on the availability of

HSDN please contact the DHS Intelligence Officer embedded in the fusion center located in the Tribe's state.

IC Tradecraft Standards for Analysts Workshop

This analytic tradecraft workshop, designed specifically for managers, focuses on effective writing of I&A intelligence products using the analytic standards established by the Office of the Director of National Intelligence's IC Directive 203, Analytic Standards. Analysts learn the eight standards of analytic tradecraft and practice applying them through a series of hands-on exercises.

Managing Analysis Workshop

This analytic tradecraft workshop, designed specifically for managers, focuses on improving analytic tradecraft through a deeper understanding and application of the analytic standards. Managers explore best practices for fostering quality analytic production in their units.

Mid-Level Intelligence and Threat Analysis Course

This ITB in-resident course provides experienced DHS intelligence professionals the opportunity to expand and enhance knowledge and skills critical to their performance and to the success of the Intelligence Enterprise (IE). The course is designed to ensure maximum student involvement. With intra-departmental participation, there is ample opportunity for students to participate in instruction, table-top exercises, site visits, and to share individual experiences and practices from their home components/organizations.

This curriculum is aligned with DHS core performance competencies and with the following tradecraft and core competencies from the IC Analytic Framework: analysis, community fundamentals, engagement and integration, critical thinking, leadership, and communication. Students are evaluated through a written test, practical exercises, instructor evaluation, and peer evaluations.

Open Source Practitioners Course (OSINT)

This ITB entry level mobile training and distance learning course is designed for DHS IE, federal, state, local, tribal, and territorial intelligence/law enforcement professionals and first preventer/first responder personnel.

This course enables students to define the Open Source landscape, conduct open source research, assess the utility of open source tools, and utilize various consolidated research resources. Students are evaluated through practical exercises and instructor evaluation.

Principles of Intelligence Writing and Briefing

This ITB entry level mobile training and distance learning course, designed for DHS analysts, introduces writing and briefing techniques within the IE and provides a foundation in communication principles: close reading, analytical writing, and effective briefing. Throughout the course, students apply learned skills by preparing finished written products and briefs via homeland security-based case studies.

Regional Analytic Advisor Plan (RAAP)

This exchange among fusion center analysts, SLTT partners, and Regional Analytic Advisors builds analytic centers of excellence, ensuring the highest quality intelligence support to SLTT partners throughout the Homeland Security Enterprise. For more information or questions, contact IA.RAAP@hq.dhs.gov.

State and Major Urban Area Fusion Centers

Fusion Centers serve as primary focal points of information sharing between federal, state, local, tribal, and territorial governments. Fusion Centers support the receipt, analysis, gathering, and sharing of threat-related information between the federal government and partners at all levels of government. Fusion Centers are owned and operated by State and local entities.

Fusion Centers are uniquely situated to empower frontline law enforcement, public safety, fire service, emergency response, public health, and private sector security personnel to understand local implications of national intelligence, thus enabling Tribal officials to better protect their communities. For assistance in developing a partnership with their local Fusion Center, tribes may contact FusionCenterSupport@HQ.DHS.GOV.

Vulnerabilities and Threat Risk Assessment (VTRA) Course

This ITB entry-level mobile training and distance learning course, designed for DHS analysts, introduces students to domestic and transnational threats facing the Homeland culminating in the creation of a vulnerability and risk assessment. Students will develop an understanding of how to evaluate threats, identify vulnerabilities in an area of responsibility, and assess threats to vulnerabilities to create risk assessments. Throughout the course, students are provided the opportunity to apply the lessons they have learned through a number of practical exercises designed to enhance their skill in creating vulnerability, threat, and risk assessments. Student knowledge is assessed through written products and briefings.

U.S. Immigration and Customs Enforcement (ICE)

U.S. Immigration and Customs Enforcement (ICE) is the principal investigative arm of the U.S. Department of Homeland Security (DHS) and the second largest investigative agency in the federal government. ICE was created in 2003 through a merger of the investigative and interior enforcement elements of the former U.S. Customs Service and the Immigration and Naturalization Service. ICE now has more than 20,000 employees in more than 400 offices in all 50 states and 48 foreign countries.

The agency has an annual budget of $5.4 billion for the 2013 fiscal year, primarily devoted to two operational directorates – Homeland Security Investigations (HSI) and Enforcement and Removal Operations (ERO). A third directorate, Management and Administration (M&A), is charged with providing professional management and mission support to advance the ICE mission.

ICE's primary mission is to promote homeland security and public safety through the criminal and civil enforcement of federal laws governing customs, international trade and immigration. This mission is executed through the enforcement of more than 400 federal statutes.

Office of State, Local and Tribal Coordination (OSLTC)

The ICE Office of State, Local and Tribal Coordination (OSLTC) is responsible for building and improving relationships and coordinating partnership activities for multiple stakeholders – including state, local and tribal governments, as well as law enforcement agencies/groups and non-governmental organizations.

OSLTC performs the following functions in support of the ICE mission:

- Fosters and sustains relationships with officials in federal, state, and local governments;
- Coordinates with state, local, and tribal law enforcement as they identify community challenges and explains the partnership services ICE can provide to meet those challenges;
- Provides information and seeks input from community groups and non-governmental organizations; and
- Builds awareness and understanding of the ICE Agreements of Cooperation in Communities to Enhance Safety and Security (ICE ACCESS: www.ice.gov/access) program.

Blue Campaign to Combat Human Trafficking

Blue Campaign is the unified voice for the DHS' efforts to combat human trafficking. Working in collaboration with law enforcement, government, non-governmental and private organizations, Blue Campaign strives to protect the basic right of freedom and to bring those who exploit human lives to justice.

DHS is responsible for investigating human trafficking, arresting traffickers, and protecting victims. DHS also provides immigration relief to foreign-born victims of human trafficking. The public is encouraged to report all suspicious activity to ICE at (866) DHS-2ICE (1-866-347-2423).

Informational material on human trafficking is produced in a variety of languages and is available to law enforcement, NGOs, and international organizations and includes the following: a public service announcement, human trafficking brochure in several languages, and human trafficking indicator wallet cards that highlight differences between smuggling and trafficking and identify key signals for recognizing a trafficking victim. For more information, visit http://www.dhs.gov/topic/human-trafficking.

If You Have the Right to Work, Don't Let Anyone Take it Away Poster

This poster serves as a resource and contains Department of Justice information regarding discrimination in the workplace. See http://www.uscis.gov/files/nativedocuments/e-verify-swa-right-to-work.pdf.

Law Enforcement Information Sharing Services (ICE Pattern Analysis and Information Collection System)

The Law Enforcement Information Sharing (LEIS) Service is a web-based data exchange platform, hosted by the Department of Homeland Security, that allows law enforcement agencies to rapidly share and access data related to criminal and national security investigations. The automated LEIS Service offers a more efficient system for requesting and sharing investigative information, helping investigators to more quickly identify patterns, connections, and relationships between individuals and criminal organizations.

The LEIS Service currently provides federal, state, local, tribal, and international law enforcement agency partners with access to more than 2.6 million subject records related to persons of interest, including suspects in child pornography, drug smuggling, immigration fraud, alien smuggling, and a wide range of other cases.

Law Enforcement Support Center (LESC)

The LESC is a national enforcement operations facility administered by ICE, the largest investigative agency in DHS. The LESC is a single national point of contact that provides timely immigration status and identity information and real-time assistance to local, state, and federal law enforcement agencies on aliens suspected, arrested, or convicted of criminal activity. Located in Williston, Vermont, the LESC operates around the clock 365 days a year. State and local law enforcement officers seeking information about aliens are the primary users of the LESC.

The LESC also receives queries from federal, state, and local correctional and court systems seeking information about individuals in custody or encountered elsewhere in the criminal justice system. Law enforcement officers have immediate access to alien records entered with the National Crime Information Center and certain immigration information from alien files maintained by DHS. Records can be accessed by using the formatted Immigration Alien Query screen incorporated within each state's law enforcement communications system.

Resources for Victims of Human Trafficking and Other Crimes

USCIS has a variety of resources for victims of human trafficking including Immigration Remedies for Trafficking Victims, Immigration Options for Victims of Crimes (in Spanish, Russian, and English), and a 'How Do I' Guide for non-immigrants. To access these and other resources, please visit the "Resources" section of www.uscis.gov.

ICE recognizes that severe consequences of human trafficking continue even after the perpetrators have been arrested and held accountable. ICE's Victim Assistance Program helps coordinate services to help human trafficking victims, such as crisis intervention, counseling and emotional support. Please visit the ICE, Investigations, Human Trafficking Public Awareness site at http://www.ice.gov/human-trafficking/.

Victim Assistance Program (VAP)

The VAP provides information and assistance to victims of federal crimes, including human trafficking, child exploitation, human rights abuse, and white collar crime. VAP also provides information to victims on post-correctional release or removal of criminal aliens from ICE custody.

VAP has developed informational brochures on human trafficking victim assistance, crime victims' rights, white collar crime, and the victim notification program. For further information, please contact VAP at 1-866-872-4973.

Homeland Security Investigations (HSI) Tipline Unit

The HSI Tipline is a 24x7 centralized intake center established to receive tips from the public and law enforcement. The Tipline receives, analyzes, documents, and disseminates tip information regarding more than 400 laws enforced by DHS. Highly trained investigative analysts have the knowledge and experience to quickly disseminate actionable leads to the responsible DHS field office, both in the United States and to HSI Attaché offices around the world.

With broad access to law enforcement and commercial computer databases, Tipline analysts can enhance tip information prior to forwarding to the responsible field office. With real-time access to interpreter services, information can be collected using more than 300 languages. The Tipline also has the ability to quickly connect federal, state, local, and tribal law enforcement officers with their local HSI duty agent. To contact the HSI Tipline, call toll free (866) 347-2423 or use the internet-based HSI Tip Form at www.ice.gov/tips. Also available is a —widget that can be placed on the websites of partner organizations and companies to allow for one-click access to the HSI Tip Form.

Office of Infrastructure Protection (IP)

Critical infrastructure is the backbone of our Nation's economy, security, and health. We know it as the power we use in our homes, the water we drink, the transportation that moves us, and the communication systems we rely on to stay in touch with friends and family.

DHS is working to raise awareness about the importance of our nation's critical infrastructure and to strengthen our ability to protect it. The Department oversees programs and resources that foster public-private partnerships, enhance protective programs, and build national resiliency to withstand natural disasters and terrorist threats. For more information, visit www.dhs.gov/criticalinfrastructure.

Active Shooter Resources

Active Shooter Resources include a desk reference guide, a reference poster, and a pocket-size reference card to address how employees, managers, training staff, and human resources personnel can mitigate the risk of and appropriately react in the event of an active shooter situation.

The desk reference guide, pocket card and poster are available on the following websites (Content also available in Spanish):

- http://www.dhs.gov/xlibrary/assets/active_shooter_poster.pdf
- http://www.dhs.gov/xlibrary/assets/active_shooter_booklet.pdf
- http://www.dhs.gov/xlibrary/assets/active_shooter_pocket_card.pdf
- http://www.dhs.gov/xlibrary/assets/active-shooter-poster-spanish.pdf
- http://www.dhs.gov/xlibrary/assets/active-shooter-pocket-spanish.pdf

For more information, please contact the Commercial Facilities SSA at CFSTeam@dhs.gov.

Business Continuity Planning Suite

IP, as the Critical Manufacturing SSA, developed an introductory Business Continuity Planning Suite to assist small to medium-sized companies in reducing the potential impact of a disruption to business. The Suite includes Business Continuity Planning Training, Business Continuity and Disaster Recovery Plan Generators, and a Business Continuity Plan Validation.

The planning suite can be located at http://www.ready.gov/business-continuity-planning-suite. For more information, contact the NPPD/IP Critical Manufacturing SSA at CM-SSA@hq.dhs.gov.

Critical Infrastructure and Key Resource (CIKR) Asset Protection Technical Assistance Program (CAPTAP)

CAPTAP is a weeklong course designed to assist state and local law enforcement, first responders, emergency management, and other homeland security officials in understanding the steps necessary to develop and implement a comprehensive CI protection program in their respective jurisdictions through the facilitated sharing of best practices and lessons learned. This includes understanding processes, methodologies, and resources necessary to identify, assess, prioritize, and protect CI assets, as well as those capabilities necessary to prevent and respond to incidents, should they occur.

Through a partnership with the National Guard Bureau (NGB), the U.S. Army Research, Development and Engineering Command (RDECOM), and the DHS Office of Infrastructure Protection's (IP) Infrastructure Information Collection Division (IICD), this service also provides web-based and instructor-led training on Protected Critical Infrastructure Information (PCII) and the use of the *Automated Critical Asset Management System* (ACAMS) and *Integrated Common Analytical Viewer* (iCAV) tools.

For more information, visit www.dhs.gov/files/programs/gc_1195679577314.shtm or contact IICD Training Team at TrainingHelp@hq.dhs.gov.

Critical Infrastructure Toolkit
The Critical Infrastructure Toolkit is a resource for infrastructure owners and operators at the local and regional levels to enhance their ability to prepare for, protect against, respond to, and recover from the full range of 21st-century threats and hazards.

The interactive resource includes a brief overview video introduction to content and critical infrastructure definitions; a guide for conducting tabletop exercises to evaluate infrastructure protection and resilience plans; exercise scenarios; and how to engage in infrastructure protection partnerships.

Links to online reference materials, training resources, and videos related to infrastructure protection and resilience are also included in the toolkit, found here:
http://emilms.fema.gov/IS921/921_Toolkit/index.htm.
Implementing Critical Infrastructure Protection Programs, a web-based training offered through the FEMA Emergency Management Institute, can be found here:
http://training.fema.gov/EMIWeb/IS/IS921.asp.

For more information about the NPPD/IP Sector Outreach and Programs Division training course, please contact: IP_Education@hq.dhs.gov.

Dams Sector Crisis Management Handbook
The Dams Sector Crisis Management Handbook provides owners/operators with information relating to emergency response and preparedness issues and includes recommendations for developing emergency action plans and site recovery plans. The handbook is available at
http://training.fema.gov/EMIWeb/IS/IS860a/CIKR/assets/DamsSectorCrisisManagementHandbook.pdf.
For more information, please contact the Dams SSA at Dams@hq.dhs.gov.

Emergency Services Self-Assessment Tool (ESSAT)
ESSAT is a secure, web-based application that enables public and private entities to perform risk assessments of specialized assets and systems, as well as multiple systems in a particular region, through voluntary and interactive stakeholder involvement. It allows for a coordinated effort among

sector partners by collecting and sharing common risk gaps, obstacles, and protective measures. The tool benefits individual partners and collective disciplines, and supports sector-wide risk management efforts. For more information, please contact the Emergency Services SSA at ESSTeam@hq.dhs.gov.

Food and Agriculture Sector Criticality Assessment Tool (FASCAT)

FASCAT is a web-based tool used to identify specific systems-based criteria, unique for the Food and Agriculture Sector and utilized for HITRAC data call submissions and identification of infrastructure critical systems for industry owners and operators. For more information, visit www.foodshield.org, or contact Food.AG@hq.dhs.gov.

Guide to Critical Infrastructure and Key Resources (CIKR) Protection at the State, Regional, Local, Tribal, & Territorial Level

This guide outlines the attributes, capabilities, needs, and processes that a State or local government entity should include in establishing its own CI protection function that integrates with the National Infrastructure Protection Plan (NIPP) and accomplishes the desired local benefits. This document is available by contacting the NIPP Program Management Office at NIPP@dhs.gov.

Homeland Security Information Network-Critical Sectors (HSIN-CS)

HSIN-CS is the primary information-sharing platform between the critical infrastructure sector stakeholders. With a library of products that increases on an average of every 2 hours, HSIN-CS enables federal, state, local, and private sector critical infrastructure owners and operators to communicate, coordinate, and share sensitive and sector-relevant information to protect their critical assets, systems, functions, and networks, at no charge to sector stakeholders.

To request access to HSIN-CS, please contact CIKRISEAccess@hq.dhs.gov. When requesting access, please indicate the critical infrastructure sector to which your company belongs and include your name, company, official email address, and supervisor's name and phone number.

Infrastructure Protection Program

The overarching goal of the National Infrastructure Protection Plan (NIPP) is to build a safer, more secure, and more resilient America by preventing, deterring, neutralizing, or mitigating the effects of a terrorist attack or natural disaster, and to strengthen national preparedness, response, and recovery in the event of an emergency. The NIPP was developed by critical infrastructure partners including federal departments and agencies, state and local government agencies, and private sector entities.

First released in 2006, the revised NIPP integrates the concepts of resilience and protection, and broadens the focus of NIPP-related programs and activities to an all-hazards environment. DHS oversees NIPP management and implementation.

More information on the Office of Infrastructure Protection activities can be located at http://www.dhs.gov/office-infrastructure-protection.

Infrastructure Protection Sector-Specific Table Top Exercise Program (SSTEP) for the Commercial Facilities Retail/Lodging Subsectors and Sports Leagues/Public Assembly Subsectors

These tools are unclassified, adaptable and immediately deployable exercises which focus on information sharing that can be utilized by retail/lodging and outdoor venues/sports leagues organizations at their facilities.

In addition to the exercise scenario and slide presentation, users will find adaptable invitational communication tools, as well as the after action report template and participant surveys which will assist in incorporating change and developing improvement plans accordingly. The Retail/Lodging and Sports Leagues/Outdoor Venues SSTEPs will allow participants the opportunity to gain an understanding of issues faced prior to, during, and after a terrorist threat/attack and the coordination with other entities, both private and government, regarding a specific facility. For more information, please contact the NPPD/IP Commercial Facilities SSA at CFSTeam@dhs.gov.

IS-906 Workplace Security Awareness

This online training provides guidance to individuals and organizations on how to improve security in the workplace. The course promotes workplace security practices applicable across all 18 critical infrastructure sectors. Threat scenarios include: Access & Security Control, Criminal & Suspicious Activities, Workplace Violence, and Cyber Threats.

The training may be accessed on the Federal Emergency Management Agency Emergency Management Institute Web site, located at http://training.fema.gov/EMIWeb/IS/IS906.asp. For more information about NPPD/IP Sector Outreach and Programs Division training courses, contact IP_Education@hq.dhs.gov.

IS-907 - Active Shooter: What You Can Do

This online training provides guidance to individuals, including managers and employees, so that they can prepare to respond to an active shooter situation. The course is self-paced and takes about 45 minutes to complete. This comprehensive cross-sector training is appropriate for a broad audience regardless of knowledge and skill level. The training uses interactive scenarios and videos to illustrate how individuals who become involved in an active shooter situation should react.

Topics within the course include:
- The actions one should take when confronted with an active shooter and responding law enforcement officials.
- How to recognize potential indicators of workplace violence.
- The actions one should take to prevent and prepare for potential active shooter incidents.
- How to manage an active shooter incident.

This course also features interactive knowledge reviews, a final exam, and additional resources. A certificate is given to participants who complete the entire course. The training may be accessed on the

Federal Emergency Management Agency Emergency Management Institute Web site, located at http://training.fema.gov/EMIWeb/IS/IS907.asp.

For more information about Office of Infrastructure Protection training courses, please contact IPEducation@hq.dhs.gov.

IS-921 Implementing Critical Infrastructure Protection Programs

This training is designed to provide the tools and techniques needed by individuals with Critical Infrastructure Protection responsibilities for both government and private sector organizations at the local, state, regional and federal levels. The content covers a range of topics including: forming partnerships, sharing information, managing risk, and ensuring continuous improvement for critical infrastructure protection and resilience programs.

The three-hour training carries .3 continuing education credits and can be accessed free of charge by visiting http://emilms.fema.gov/IS921/index.htm.

For more information about the NPPD/IP Sector Outreach and Programs Division training course, please contact IP_Education@hq.dhs.gov.

Improvised Explosive Device (IED) Counterterrorism Workshop

This workshop provides exposure to key elements of the IED threat, surveillance detection methods, and soft target awareness. The workshop illustrates baseline awareness/prevention activities that reduce vulnerabilities along with information sharing resources to improve preparedness. The workshop improves critical infrastructure owners' and operators' understanding of new IED threats and the terrorist attack cycle.

State/local law enforcement and public/private sector stakeholders are encouraged to attend. This eight-hour workshop can accommodate 250 participants. To request training, contact your State Homeland Security Advisor.

Protective Measures Course

This course provides executive, management, and operations level personnel in both the public and private sectors with an overview of information regarding threat analysis, terrorist planning, facility vulnerability analysis, and protective measures and strategies which can be utilized to mitigate risk and reduce vulnerabilities within their unique sectors. This two-day course can accommodate 75 participants. To request training, contact your State Homeland Security Advisor.

Surveillance Detection Course for Law Enforcement and Security Professionals

This course provides instruction on how to detect hostile surveillance conducted against critical infrastructure. By exploring surveillance techniques, tactics, and procedures from a hostile perspective, attendees expand their ability to proactively detect, deter, prevent, and respond to an IED threat. Law enforcement and private sector security professionals are encouraged to attend. This three-day course can accommodate 25 participants. To request training, contact your State Homeland Security Advisor.

Improvised Explosive Device (IED) Awareness/Bomb Threat Management Workshop

This workshop improves facility owners', operators', and security managers' ability to manage IED threats by highlighting specific safety precautions associated with explosive incidents and bomb threats. The workshop reinforces an integrated approach that combines training, planning, and equipment acquisition to maximize available resources for bomb threat management. Public and private sector representatives knowledgeable in regional emergency management procedures are encouraged to attend. This four-hour course can accommodate 50 participants. To request training, contact your State Homeland Security Advisor.

Improvised Explosive Device (IED) Search Procedures Workshop

This workshop improves participants' understanding of IED awareness, IED prevention measures, and planning protocols to detect IEDs by reviewing specific search techniques. This workshop will enable public and private sector representatives to reduce vulnerability to and mitigate the effects of IED attacks. Law enforcement and private sector security personnel responsible for bomb threat management planning/response are encouraged to attend. This eight-hour course can accommodate 40 participants. To request training, contact your State Homeland Security Advisor.

National Capabilities Analysis Database (NCAD)

NCAD uses a task-based methodology to provide a uniform analysis of bomb squad, dive team, explosive detection canine team, and SWAT (special weapons and tactics) team capabilities throughout the United States. NCAD utilizes data obtained from on-site unit surveys and assessments, and allows OBP to produce formal assessment reports that measure readiness and training levels and track the assets and equipment required for effective responses to IED threats. This integrated information provides a snapshot of national IED preparedness that drives resource allocation and capability enhancements. For more information, contact OBP@dhs.gov.

Multi-Jurisdiction Improvised Explosive Device Security Planning (MJIEDSP)

The MJIEDSP process assists high-risk multi-jurisdiction areas in developing a detailed IED security plan that outlines specific bombing prevention actions that reduce vulnerability and mitigate the risk of IED attacks within these sections. An effective response to an IED incident requires the close coordination of many different public safety and law enforcement organizations and disciplines. OBP works closely with each MJIEDSP community to provide expertise on operational planning and the development of steady-state and threat-initiated actions to protect critical infrastructure in the region.

Upon completion of the MJIEDSP Workshop, an analysis is compiled and presented to regional stakeholders to serve as a catalyst for adding an IED response annex to their existing emergency management plans. For more information, contact OBP@dhs.gov.

Bomb-making Materials Awareness Program (BMAP)

BMAP is a collaborative effort between IP and the Federal Bureau of Investigation (FBI) to heighten public and private sector awareness of IEDs and Homemade Explosives (HMEs). BMAP provides materials and training to local law enforcement agencies to assist them in conducting outreach to private sector businesses within their jurisdictions that manufacture, distribute, or sell products that contain HME precursor materials.

BMAP outreach materials are provided by law enforcement to local businesses to help employees identify suspicious purchasing behavior of relevant HME precursor materials and critical IED components, such as electronics, that could indicate bomb-making activity. For more information, contact OBP@dhs.gov.

Technical Resource for Incident Prevention (TRIP*wire*)

TRIP*wire* is the information-sharing network for bomb squad, law enforcement, and other emergency services personnel to learn about current terrorist IED tactics, techniques, and procedures, including design and emplacement considerations.

Developed and maintained by OBP the system combines expert analyses and reports with relevant documents, images, and videos gathered directly from terrorist sources to help law enforcement anticipate, identify, and prevent IED incidents. For more information, contact TRIPWIRE@hq.dhs.gov.

Protective Security Advisor (PSA) Program

Established in 2004, the PSA Program proactively engages with State, local, tribal and territorial (SLTT) government missions' partners and members of the private sector stakeholder community to protect the Nation's critical infrastructure.

The PSA Program's critical infrastructure protection mission is comprised of five mission areas to: plan, coordinate and conduct security surveys and assessments; plan and conduct outreach activities; support National Special Security Events (NSSEs) and Special Event Assessment Rating (SEAR) events; respond to incidents; and coordinate and support Improvised Explosive Device (IED) Awareness and Risk Mitigation Training. To accomplish these missions, PSAs utilize two cross-cutting activities, including field-level coordination and information sharing.

Private sector owners and operators interested in contacting their PSA should contact the DHS Protective Security Coordination Division (PSCD) Operations Staff at PSCDOperations@hq.dhs.gov or (703) 235-9349.

Enhanced Critical Infrastructure Protection Program (ECIP) Security Survey

The Enhanced Critical Infrastructure Protection initiative is a voluntary program consisting of security surveys and outreach. PSAs conduct on-site security surveys to assess the overall security posture of the Nation's most critical infrastructure facilities. Collected findings are compiled in a report and provided to asset owner/operators, to include Protective Measures Index (PMI) and Resilience Index (RI) interactive dashboards. Simultaneous outreach efforts provide awareness of potential threats/vulnerabilities and associated protective measures, in addition to training and exercise programs.

Regional Resiliency Assessment Program (RRAP)

The Regional Resiliency Assessment Program is a cooperative, non-regulatory, IP-led assessment of specific critical infrastructure and regional analysis of the surrounding critical infrastructure. The RRAP focuses on infrastructure systems within a designated geographic area and addresses a wide range of hazards that could have regionally and nationally significant consequences.

The RRAP identifies critical infrastructure and key resources dependencies, interdependencies, cascading effects, resiliency characteristics, regional capabilities, and security gaps. The analysis details the risk and consequences of an incident or attack, and the integrated preparedness and protection capabilities of the affected CI owners and operators, local law enforcement, and emergency response organizations.

Results can be applied to enhance the overall security posture of the facilities, surrounding communities, and geographic region using risk-based investments in equipment, planning, training, processes, procedures and resources. Additional information on this program can be located at http://www.dhs.gov/regional-resiliency-assessment-program.

Regional Resiliency Assessment Program (RRAP) Discussion Based Exercises

These exercises are offered to those jurisdictions participating in the RRAP. The core component of these efforts will be a capstone Tabletop Exercise (TTX) delivered in approximately the one-year post-Resiliency Analysis delivery timeframe. The core objective of this TTX will be to determine changes to a jurisdiction's/sector's overall Resiliency Baseline due to the implementation of suggested protective measures highlighted by the RRAP process.

In the intervening year, the Stakeholder Readiness and Exercise Team works with the RRAP exercise planning group to deliver other requested preparatory activities, such as workshops, to help shape the capstone TTX. For more information, please contact the Office of Infrastructure Protection Sector Outreach and Programs Division at SOPDExecSec@dhs.gov.

Risk Self-Assessment Tool for Stadiums and Arenas, Performing Art Centers, Lodging, Convention Centers, Racetracks, and Theme Parks

The Risk Self-Assessment Tool (RSAT) is a secure, web-based application designed to assist managers of public assembly facilities with the identification and management of security vulnerabilities to reduce risk to their facilities. The RSAT application uses facility input in combination with threat and consequence estimates to conduct a comprehensive risk assessment and provides users with options for consideration to improve the security posture of their facility. It is also accompanied by a Fact Sheet/Brochure. For more information, please contact the NPPD/IP Commercial Facilities SSA at CFSTeam@dhs.gov or RSAT@hq.dhs.gov.

State and Local Implementation Snapshot

In accordance with the National Infrastructure Protection Plan (NIPP), as well as the requirements identified in the Homeland Security Grant Program, state and tribal governments are responsible for developing, implementing, and sustaining a statewide/regional critical infrastructure protection program.

The processes necessary to implement the NIPP risk management framework at the state and/or regional level, including urban areas, should become a component of the state's overarching homeland security program. This two-page snapshot presents information on a variety of resources available to support State/local and tribal critical infrastructure protection efforts. For more information, see http://www.dhs.gov/xlibrary/assets/nipp_state_local_snapshot.pdf.

Suspicious Activity Reporting for Critical Infrastructure Tool
This tool is a standardized means by which critical infrastructure stakeholders can report suspicious or unusual activities to the government via sector portals on the Homeland Security Information Network-Critical Sectors (HSIN-CS). Reports submitted to the tool are reviewed by the National Infrastructure Coordinating Center (NICC), shared with appropriate government recipients, redacted, and posted to HSIN-CS. To request access to HSIN-CS, please contact HSINCS@dhs.gov.

The Evolving Threat: What You Can Do
This webinar discusses the latest intelligence analyzed by the DHS Office of Intelligence and Analysis (I&A), and consists of a brief synopsis of evolving threats, followed by a protective measures presentation. Additionally, the protective measures portion of the webinar is available at https://connect.HSIN.gov/p55204456. For more information, please contact the Commercial Facilities SSA at CFSTeam@dhs.gov.

Webinar: The Ready Responder Program for the Emergency Services Sector
This one-hour web-based seminar focuses on first responder preparedness and best practices and how the Ready Responder program contributes to a safer, more secure and resilient America. The webinar is available on the Homeland Security Information Sharing – Critical Sectors (HSIN-CS) Emergency Services Sector portal. For access and more information, contact the NPPD/IP Emergency Services Sector at ESSTeam@hq.dhs.gov.

Office of Emergency Communications (OEC)

Established by Congress in 2007 in response to communications challenges witnessed during the attacks on September 11, 2001 and during Hurricane Katrina, the DHS **Office of Emergency Communications (OEC)** partners with emergency communications personnel and government officials at all levels of government to lead the nationwide effort to improve emergency communications capabilities.

On July 6, 2012, Executive Order 13618 was issued by President Obama to update and clarify national security and emergency preparedness (NS/EP) communications responsibilities for the federal government. As a result, DHS has realigned programs within OEC and the former National Communications System (NCS) to lead the Department's support for emergency communications and NS/EP communications programs. The combined services of OEC's traditional support for interoperable communications with NCS' technical capabilities for NS/EP communications result in a comprehensive office to address all emergency communications issues.

SAFECOM
SAFECOM is a stakeholder-driven program that is led by an Executive Committee (EC), in support of the Emergency Response Council (ERC)—groups that are primarily composed of State, tribal, and local emergency responders and intergovernmental and national public safety communications associations. Both groups regularly convene to discuss interoperability, emergency communications, and provide input on the challenges, needs, and best practices of emergency responders. OEC develops policy, guidance, and future initiatives by drawing on EC and ERC member expertise, best practices and recommendations. For more information, please visit www.safecomprogram.gov.

Statewide Communication Interoperability Plans (SCIPs)
SCIPs are locally-driven, multi-jurisdictional, and multi-disciplinary statewide strategic plans to enhance emergency communications. The SCIP provides strategic direction and alignment for those responsible for interoperable communications at the State, tribal, regional, and local levels.

These strategic plans outline and define the current and future vision for communications interoperability within the State or territory. They also align emergency response agencies with the goals, objectives, and initiatives for achieving that vision. SCIPs are living documents that are typically updated on an annual basis, or as frequently as needed. For more information, please visit www.dhs.gov/statewide-communication-interoperability-plans.

Interoperable Communications Technical Assistance Program (ICTAP)
The ICTAP provides direct support to state, tribal, and local emergency responders and government officials through the development and delivery of training, tools, and onsite assistance to advance public safety interoperable communications capabilities. For more information on technical assistance service offerings, see www.publicsafetytools.info.

The Government Emergency Telecommunications Service (GETS)

GETS supports federal, state, tribal, and local government, industry, and non-governmental organization (NGO) personnel in performing their NS/EP missions.

GETS provides emergency access and priority processing in the local and long distance segments of the Public Switched Telephone Network (PSTN). It is intended to be used in an emergency or crisis situation when the PSTN is congested and the probability of completing a call over normal or other alternate telecommunication means has significantly decreased. For more information on how to obtain a GETS card, see www.gets.ncs.gov.

Wireless Priority Service (WPS)

WPS is a priority calling capability that greatly increases the probability of call completion during an NS/EP event while using a cellular phone. To make a WPS call, the user must first have the WPS feature added to his/her cellular service. Once established, the caller can dial ✳272 plus the destination telephone number to place an emergency wireless call.

WPS and its companion priority service, GETS, are requested through a secure on-line system. For more information on how to obtain WPS, see www.wps.ncs.gov.

Telecommunications Service Priority (TSP)

TSP is a program that authorizes NS/EP organizations to receive priority treatment for vital voice and data circuits or other telecommunications services. As a result of hurricanes, floods, earthquakes, and other natural or man-made disasters, telecommunications service vendors frequently experience a surge in requests for new services and requirements to restore existing services.

The TSP Program provides service vendors a Federal Communications Commission (FCC) mandate to prioritize requests by identifying those services critical to NS/EP. A TSP assignment ensures that it will receive priority attention by the service vendor before any non-TSP service consistent with the prioritization hierarchy set forth in FCC rules. For more information on TSP enrollment, visit www.tsp.ncs.gov.

Regional Coordination Program

The Regional Coordination Program aligns with the 10 Federal Emergency Management Agency regions. Each region is represented by an OEC Regional Coordinator. The Regional Coordinator of each region drives OEC's mission by supporting the efforts of federal, state, tribal, and local agencies to build and improve emergency communications capabilities across their regions; providing OEC with feedback and assessments of emergency communications activities, accomplishments, issues, gaps, and constraints across the nation; and successfully advocating for identified OEC initiatives, programs, and activities. To identify your Regional Coordinator, visit www.dhs.gov/oec-regional-coordination-program.

Southwest Border Communications Working Group (SWBCWG)

The SWBCWG serves as a forum for federal, state, tribal, and local agencies in Arizona, California, New Mexico, and Texas to share information on common issues, to collaborate on existing and planned activities, and to facilitate federal involvement in multi-agency projects within the Southwest Border Region.

The SWBCWG aims to enhance communications operability and interoperability, to effectively use the region's available critical communications infrastructure resources, and to ensure that programs continue to meet the stakeholders' needs. For more information on the SWBCWG, e-mail oec@dhs.gov.

Office of Health Affairs (OHA)

The Office of Health Affairs (OHA) serves as DHS's principal authority for all medical and health issues. OHA provides medical, public health, and scientific expertise in support of the Department of Homeland Security mission to prepare for, respond to, and recover from all threats. OHA serves as the principal advisor to the Secretary and the Federal Emergency Management Agency (FEMA) Administrator on medical and public health issues. OHA leads the Department's workforce health protection and medical oversight activities. The office also leads and coordinates the Department's biological and chemical defense activities and provides medical and scientific expertise to support the Department's preparedness and response efforts.

Guidance for Protecting Responders' Health During the First Week Following A Wide-Area Aerosol Anthrax Attack

DHS has issued guidance, based on a federal interagency working group effort, to educate first responders on protective actions they should take in the event of a wide-area anthrax release. The guidance, which is non-binding, provides recommendations for responders risking high, moderate, and limited exposure based on their expected activities and their potential to travel through the affected area in the immediate aftermath of an attack. For more information, see http://www.dhs.gov/publication/protecting-responders-health-after-wide-area-aerosol-anthrax-attack, or contact Healthaffairs@dhs.gov.

National Biosurveillance Integration Center (NBIC) Strategic Plan

Biosurveillance plays an important role in early detection of naturally-occurring, accidental, or deliberate biological events. Early detection allows for an early response, limiting the spread and effects of such events. The mission of NBIC is to integrate biosurveillance information in order to enable early warning and shared situational awareness.

The NBIC Strategic Plan provides an overview of national biosurveillance and current NBIC operations, then outlines the goals and objectives required to achieve its mission over the next five years. For more information, see https://www.dhs.gov/sites/default/files/publications/nbic-strategic-plan-public-2012.pdf, or contact Healthaffairs@dhs.gov.

Planning for 2009 H1N1 Influenza: A Preparedness Guide for Small Business

DHS, the Centers for Disease Control, and the Small Business Administration developed this guide to help small businesses understand what impact a new influenza virus, like the 2009 H1N1 flu, might have on their operations, and the importance of a written plan for guiding businesses through a possible pandemic. For more information, see http://www.flu.gov/professional/business/smallbiz.html, or contact IP_Education@hq.dhs.gov.

Privacy Office

The **DHS Privacy Office** sustains privacy protections and the transparency of government operations while supporting the DHS mission. The DHS Privacy Office ensures that DHS programs and operations comply with federal privacy laws and policies. Members of the public can contact the Privacy Office with concerns or complaints regarding their privacy and activities of the Department. For more information, visit www.dhs.gov/privacy, email privacy@dhs.gov, or call (202) 343-1717.

DHS Privacy Policy Guidance

DHS privacy policy guidance informs the Department and the public about how the DHS Privacy Office implements privacy at DHS. For more information please visit http://www.dhs.gov/privacy-policy-guidance.

Privacy Impact Assessments (PIAs)

PIAs are documented decision-making tools used to identify and mitigate privacy risks at the beginning of and throughout the development life cycle of a program or system. They help the public understand what personally identifiable information (PII) the Department is collecting, why it is being collected, and how it will be used, shared, accessed, and stored. All published PIAs issued by DHS may be found here: http://www.dhs.gov/files/publications/editorial_0511.shtm.

System of Records Notices (SORNs)

SORNs provide public notice regarding personal information, including PII, collected in a system of records. SORNs explain how the information is used, retained, and may be corrected, and whether certain portions of the system are subject to Privacy Act exemptions for law enforcement or national security reasons. The Chief Privacy Officer reviews, signs, and publishes all SORNs for the Department. Copies of all DHS SORNs are available at http://www.dhs.gov/system-records-notices-sorns.

Privacy Office Reports to Congress

Privacy Office reports to Congress provide transparency into the Privacy Office's work with DHS Components, offices and programs to protect privacy. These reports include:
- DHS Privacy Office Annual Report to Congress
- Quarterly reports required under Section 803 of the Implementing Recommendations of the 9/11 Commission Report of 2007
- DHS Annual Data Mining Report

These reports are available on the DHS Privacy Office's website at http://www.dhs.gov/privacy-foia-reports.

Freedom of Information Act (FOIA)

FOIA operations promote transparency about DHS activities and help individuals understand how the Department uses information it collects about them. The Chief Privacy Officer serves as the Chief FOIA Officer.

The DHS Privacy Office coordinates and oversees Component FOIA Office operations, provides FOIA training, and prepares required annual reports on the Department's FOIA performance. The DHS Privacy Office, through its FOIA unit, also processes initial FOIA and Privacy Act disclosure requests to the Office of the Secretary (including the Military Advisor's Office and the Office of Intergovernmental Affairs), and all divisions within DHS Headquarters.

Information about FOIA and disclosure can be found at http://www.dhs.gov/landing-page/freedom-information-act-foia-and-privacy-act.

FOIA Reports
FOIA Reports provide transparency on public inspection of records activities of the Department.

- Freedom of Information Act Annual Reports.
- DHS Chief FOIA Officer's Annual Report

These reports are available on the DHS Privacy Office's website at http://www.dhs.gov/foia-library-frequently-requested-records#3.

Science and Technology Directorate (S&T)

The **Science and Technology Directorate (S&T)** manages science and technology research to protect the homeland, from development through transition for Department components and first responders. S&T's mission is to strengthen America's security and resiliency by providing knowledge products and innovative technology solutions for the Homeland Security Enterprise (HSE). For more information, visit their website at www.dhs.gov/scienceandtechnology.

FirstResponder.gov

The FirstResponder.gov mission is to provide a portal that enables federal, state, local, and tribal first responders to easily access and leverage federal web services, information on resources, products, standards, testing and evaluation, and best practices, in a collaborative environment. The portal provides first responders with information to develop or deploy technologies that would enhance homeland security. For more information, visit www.firstresponder.gov.

First Responder Communities of Practice

First Responder Communities of Practice is an online network of vetted, active, and retired first responders, emergency response professionals; and federal, state, local, or tribal Homeland Security officials sponsored by the DHS S&T's First Responders Group. Registered members of this professional network share information, ideas, and best practices, enabling them to more efficiently and effectively prepare for all hazards. For more information, visit www.firstresponder.gov or https://communities.firstresponder.gov.

Centers of Excellence (COE)

The Centers of Excellence network is an extended consortium of hundreds of universities generating ground-breaking ideas for new technologies and critical knowledge, while also relying on each other's capabilities to serve the Department's many mission needs.

All Centers of Excellence work closely with academia, industry, Department components and first-responders to develop customer-driven research solutions to 'on the ground' challenges as well as provide essential training to the next generation of homeland security experts. The research portfolio is a mix of basic and applied research addressing both short and long-term needs. The COE extended network is also available for rapid response efforts.

Managed through the Office of University Programs, the Centers of Excellence organize leading experts and researchers to conduct multidisciplinary homeland security research and education. Each center is university-led or co-led in collaboration with partners from other institutions, agencies, national laboratories, think tanks and the private sector. For more information, visit http://www.dhs.gov/files/programs/editorial_0498.shtm or http://www.dhs.gov/st-office-university-programs.

Transportation Security Administration (TSA)

Following September 11, 2001, the **Transportation Security Administration (TSA)** was created to strengthen the security of the nation's transportation systems and ensure the freedom of movement for people and commerce. Today, TSA secures the nation's airports and screens all commercial airline passengers and baggage. TSA uses a risk-based strategy and works closely with transportation, law enforcement, and intelligence communities to set the standard for excellence in transportation security.

Airspace Waivers

The Federal Aviation Administration (FAA) may impose restrictions on flight operations in certain areas of the National Airspace System, prohibiting general aviation (GA) operations, unless an airspace waiver is granted following a thorough security threat assessment. These areas are in place to mitigate the threat of an airborne attack against key assets and critical infrastructure on the ground. TSA shares the responsibility with the FAA for managing the airspace waivers process.

The TSA Office of Law Enforcement/Federal Air Marshal Service (OLE/FAMS) Flight Operations Division's Airspace Authorizations Office manages the security portion of the process and assists with the review of general aviation aircraft operators who request to enter areas of restricted airspace. Pilots must possess a copy of the waiver when filing a flight plan and during flight operations. For more information, call 571-227-2071.

Counterterrorism Guides

TSA has created four Highway Security Counterterrorism Guides—Motorcoach, School Bus Transportation, Trucking, and Infrastructure. Each guide is a pocket-sized flip chart covering the following topics: Pre-Incident Indicators, Targets and Threats, Tactics, Prevention/Mitigation, Security Exercises, Chemical Biological Radiological Nuclear (CBRN), Licensing and Identification and Points of Contact.

I.   Motorcoach

- Employee Guide to Motorcoach Security Brochure

- Motorcoach Awareness Poster for Terminals: "Watch for Suspicious Items"

- Motorcoach Awareness Poster for Terminals: "Watch for Suspicious Behaviors"

II.   School Bus Transportation

- Employee Guide to School Bus Security brochure

- School Transportation Employee Awareness Poster

- School Transportation Security Awareness (STSA) DVD

III. Trucking

- Security Guide for Owner-Operator Independent Drivers Association Members (OOIDA)

- Security Guide for Tank Truck Carrier Employees

- Security Guide for Private and Contract Carrier Company Employees

- Security Guide for Truck Rental Company Employees

IV. Infrastructure

- Security Guide for Infrastructure Owner/Operators

DVD-based training programs

In addition to these documents, TSA has developed two DVD-based training programs. The first is entitled *Pipelines: Countering IEDs* and is intended to familiarize pipeline company employees and contractors with the threat posed by Improvised Explosive Devices (IEDs). This DVD training employs four modules which familiarize viewers with the threat posed by IEDs, how to spot potential IEDs, how to respond to suspicious objects, and how to work with responding agencies in the event an IED is discovered or detonated on company property. This DVD incorporates interactive quizzes which can be used to test participants' knowledge at the end of each module.

The second DVD is *Protecting Pipeline Infrastructure: The Law Enforcement Role*. Identifying a gap in the existing training materials, TSA developed this DVD training program to enhance the understanding of pipeline systems and their security issues by law enforcement officials. This DVD provides a basic understanding of how pipeline systems function, the principal products they transport, as well as a description of the threats to, and vulnerabilities of, pipelines. Law enforcement officials will achieve a better understanding of the usual measures taken to protect pipelines, and actions they can take to assist in this effort during times of heightened security.

First Observer Program

The First Observer Program has been the premier anti-terrorism domain awareness training program for highway professionals to identify, observe, assess and report potential terrorist or suspicious activities and/or behaviors. Contact the Information Sharing and Analysis Center (ISAC) at 1-877-847-5510 to report any suspicious activity. First Observer training is free, and curricula are available. Contact FirstObserver@tsa.dhs.gov for more information.

Freight Rail Security Awareness Brochure

A supplemental brochure, "Freight Rail Security Awareness," is available as a PDF file and can be customized by companies to meet their needs. The CD and Brochure can be ordered by sending an email to freightrailsecurity@dhs.gov.

General Aviation (GA) Secure Hotline
TSA developed and implemented a GA hotline in partnership with the National Response Center. The GA Hotline serves as a centralized reporting system for general aviation pilots, airport operators, and maintenance technicians wishing to report suspicious activity at their airfield. To reach the hotline, call 1-866-GA-SECUR (1-866- 427-3287).

General Aviation Security Guidelines
This document constitutes a set of federally endorsed guidelines for enhancing airport security at GA facilities throughout the Nation. It is intended to provide GA airport owners, operators, and users with guidelines and recommendations that address aviation security concepts, technology, and enhancements. To view the document, visit http://www.tsa.gov/sites/default/files/assets/pdf/Intermodal/security_guidelines_for_general_aviation _airports.pdf.

Highway Government & Sector Coordinating Council
The objective of the Highway Government Coordinating Council (GCC) is to coordinate highway and motor carrier security strategies and activities, to establish policies, guidelines and standards, and to develop program metrics and performance criteria for the mode.

Highway Motor Carrier (HMC) has an active Sector Coordinating Council (SCC) for private industry to partner with senior government officials to collaborate and communicate on security initiatives designed to enhance the protection of the transportation sector's critical infrastructure and key resources. Please contact Doug Morris at doug_morris@ooida.com to become a member of SCC.

HMC Brochures
Highway Security Counterterrorism Guides, Awareness Brochures, Tip Cards, Posters, and training information can be found at www.TSA.Gov/Highway or by emailing highwaysecurity@dhs.gov for additional information.

HMC I-STEP Program
The HMC I-STEP is an interactive, tabletop exercise program designed to test, verify and measure the effectiveness of security plans and protocols of our security partners. The main benefit to conducting an HMC I-STEP is to collect information on what is currently working in the highway mode and sharing the lessons learned and best practices. I-STEP exercises are held for all highway transportation sub-modes at various locations across the U.S. and stakeholders are encouraged to attend and actively participate. Specific date and location information can be found on the HMC website.

IED Recognition and Detection for Railroad Industry Employees Training CD
TSA has produced a CD-ROM-based training program entitled, "IED Recognition and Detection for Railroad Industry Employees." This is a self-paced program that leads users through four separate modules that focus on heightening rail employees' awareness of suspicious activity. Topics include an overview of the terrorist threat, high risk targets, improvised explosive device recognition, and inspection and response procedures.

Law Enforcement Officers Flying Armed (LEOFA)/ National Law Enforcement Telecommunications System (NLETS) Program

TSA's Office of Law Enforcement/Federal Air Marshal Service (OLE/FAMS) maintains oversight of the Law Enforcement Officers Flying Armed (LEOFA) program. The program assists federal, state, local and tribal law enforcement agencies, who meet certain requirements, with the ability to travel while armed on commercial aircraft. In support of this program, OLE/FAMS provides training to qualified law enforcement agencies that are able to demonstrate a need to fly armed.

Qualified federal agencies receive a Unique Federal Agency Number (UFAN), while state, local and tribal agencies utilize the National Law Enforcement Telecommunications System (NLETS) to transmit a message to TSA in order to fly armed. For general questions or guidance related to Law Enforcement Officers flying armed, please contact the Office of Law Enforcement/Federal Air Marshal Service, Liaison Division at (703) 487-0033 or LEOFA@dhs.gov.

Recommended GA Security Action Items

TSA issued "Recommended Security Action Items for General Aviation Aircraft Operators" and "Recommended Security Action Items for Fixed Base Operators." These voluntary action items are measures that aircraft operators and fixed base operators should consider when they develop, implement or revise security plans or other efforts to enhance security. To view the two documents, visit the following links:

- http://www.tsa.gov/sites/default/files/assets/pdf/Intermodal/rec_sai_ga_ao.pdf
- http://www.tsa.gov/sites/default/files/assets/pdf/Intermodal/rec_sai_ga_fbo.pdf

TSA Pipeline Security Guidelines and Pipeline Smart Security Practice Observations

TSA has developed two significant documents to assist pipeline operators in securing their operations— the *TSA Pipeline Security Guidelines* and *Pipeline Smart Security Practice Observations*. The *Guidelines* document, which was issued in April 2011, provides explicit TSA recommendations for pipeline industry security practices.

The *Smart Practice Observations* is a tool for pipeline security professionals seeking concepts or ideas to improve their security program. This document is a compilation of the smart security practices that were observed by the Pipeline Security Division during Corporate Security Reviews and Critical Facility Inspections of pipeline companies.

TSA Website/ Highway & Motor Carrier E-mail

TSA's main portal to highway security information is our HMC website, www.tsa.gov/highway. All TSA programs and initiatives can be found and researched from this portal. Additionally, HMC uses an email address (highwaysecurity@dhs.gov) to send, receive and facilitate communications with federal, state, local, tribal and private sector stakeholders as deemed appropriate.

TSA Security Clearance

Highway and Motor Carrier Program Office (HMC) will nominate Industry officials for TSA-sponsored security clearances as part of the Private Industry Clearance Program in conjunction with the Office of Personnel Security Section (PerSecERSEC). Contact Ray Cotton at Ray.Cotton@tsa.dhs.gov.

U.S. Coast Guard (USCG)

The **U.S. Coast Guard** is one of the five armed forces of the United States and the only military organization within the Department of Homeland Security. Since 1790 the Coast Guard has safeguarded our Nation's maritime interests and environment around the world. The Coast Guard is an adaptable, responsive military force of maritime professionals whose broad legal authorities, capable assets, geographic diversity and expansive partnerships provide a persistent presence along our rivers, in the ports, littoral regions and on the high seas. Coast Guard presence and impact is local, regional, national and international. These attributes make the Coast Guard a unique instrument of maritime safety, security and environmental stewardship. For more information, visit www.uscg.mil.

America's Waterways Watch

America's Waterways Watch is a combined public outreach effort of the U.S. Coast Guard and its Reserve and Auxiliary components to encourage participants to report suspicious activity to the Coast Guard and/or other law enforcement agencies.

For more information, contact aww@uscg.mil or visit http://americaswaterwaywatch.uscg.mil. To report suspicious activity, call 877-24WATCH (877-249-2824).

U.S. Coast Guard Maritime Information eXchange ("CGMIX")

CGMIX makes U.S. Coast Guard (USCG) maritime information available to the public on the internet in the form of searchable databases. Much of the information on the CGMIX web site comes from the USCG's Marine Information for Safety and Law Enforcement (MISLE) information system. For more information see http://cgmix.uscg.mil/.

U.S. Coast Guard Navigation Center

The U.S. Coast Guard Navigation Center supports safe and efficient maritime transportation by delivering accurate and timely maritime information services and Global Position System (GPS) augmentation signals that permit high-precision positioning and navigation. For more information, visit the website at http://www.navcen.uscg.gov/or call (703) 313-5900.

Additional Resources:

Department Wide Resources

Environmental Justice Program

The Environmental Justice Program at the Department is not the responsibility of a single office, but rather a joint effort between the Office for Civil Rights and Civil Liberties (CRCL) and the Office of the Under Secretary for Management (USM)/Office of the Chief Readiness Support Officer (OCRSO) to involve component counterparts in improving recognition of environmental justice equities across their respective components. Environmental justice describes the commitment of the federal government, through its policies, programs, and activities, to avoid placing disproportionately high and adverse effects on the human health and environment of minority or low-income populations.

As described in the 2010 Quadrennial Homeland Security Review (QHSR), our Nation's vision of homeland security is a homeland safe and secure, resilient against terrorism and other hazards, and where American interests and aspirations and the American way of life can thrive. In seeking to fulfill this vision, DHS aspires to avoid burdening minority and low-income populations with a disproportionate share of any adverse human health or environmental risks associated with our efforts to secure the Nation.

DHS joins with other departments and agencies to appropriately include environmental justice practices in our larger mission efforts involving federal law enforcement and emergency response activities. For more information, go to http://www.dhs.gov/xabout/laws/editorial_0850.shtm.

Homeland Security Information Network (HSIN)

The Homeland Security Information Network is a national secure and trusted web-based portal for information sharing and collaboration between federal, state, local, tribal, territorial, private sector, and international partners engaged in the homeland security mission.

HSIN is made up of a growing network of communities, called Communities of Interest (COI). COIs are organized by state organizations, federal organizations, or mission areas, such as emergency management, law enforcement, critical sectors, and intelligence. Users can securely share within their communities or reach out to other communities as needed.

HSIN provides secure, real-time collaboration tools, including a virtual meeting space, instant messaging and document sharing. HSIN allows partners to work together instantly, regardless of their location, to communicate, collaborate, and coordinate. For more information, go to www.dhs.gov/HSIN.

The DHS Veterans Employment Program Directive 3011

This Directive reaffirms the DHS commitment to providing employment opportunities and benefits to veterans seeking federal jobs and employees returning from active military duty.

DHS believes that the expertise and experience that veterans offer DHS and its organizational elements is of significant value to the DHS mission, and fully supports the laws and regulations providing for veterans' preference in federal employment. For more information, visit **www.dhs.gov/veterans-and-homeland-security**.

Office of Biometric Identity Management (OBIM)

OBIM, formerly known as the United States Visitor and Immigrant Status Indicator Technology (US-VISIT) Program, has provided biometric and associated biographic identity verification and analysis services to the Department since 2004. OBIM supports Federal, State, local, and tribal law enforcement agencies, the law enforcement community, the Intelligence Community (IC), and international partners involved in homeland security, immigration, law enforcement, and credentialing.

The OBIM Biometric Support Center (BSC) provides expert fingerprint verification in support of stakeholder operations, including latent fingerprint identification in order to solve crimes, support terrorist investigations, and identify unknown deceased persons in support of criminal cases. For more information, please visit www.dhs.gov/us-visit-office or call (202) 298-5200.

DHS Grants

Assistance to Firefighter Grants (AFG)
A program of the Federal Emergency Management Agency, grants are awarded to fire departments to enhance their ability to protect the public and fire service personnel from fire and related hazards. Three types of grants are available—Assistance to Firefighters Grants (AFG), Staffing for Adequate Fire and Emergency Response Grants (SAFER), and Fire Prevention and Safety Grants (FP&S). For more information, visit www.fema.gov/firegrants/.

Community Assistance Program, State Support Services Element (CAP-SSSE)
The Community Assistance Program –State Support Services Element (CAP-SSSE) program derives its authority from the National Flood Insurance Act of 1968, as amended, the Flood Disaster Protection Act of 1973, and from 44 CFR Parts 59 and 60. This program provides funding to states to provide technical assistance to communities in the National Flood Insurance Program (NFIP) and to evaluate community performance in implementing NFIP floodplain management activities. In this way, CAP-SSSE helps to:

- Ensure that the flood loss reduction goals of the NFIP are met,

- Build State and community floodplain management expertise and capability, and

- Leverage State knowledge and expertise in working with their communities.

For more information, visit www.fema.gov/plan/prevent/floodplain/fema_cap-ssse.shtm.

Community Disaster Loan Program
The Community Disaster Loan Program provides funds to any eligible jurisdiction in a designated disaster area that has suffered a substantial loss of tax and other revenue. The jurisdiction must demonstrate a need for financial assistance to perform its governmental functions. For more information visit the website www.fema.gov/government/grant/fs_cdl.shtm.

Emergency Management Performance Grant (EMPG)
The purpose of the EMPG Program is to make grants to states to assist state, local, tribal and territorial governments in preparing for all hazards, as authorized by the Robert T. Stafford Disaster Relief and Emergency Assistance Act (42 U.S.C. 5121 et seq.). Title VI of the Stafford Act authorizes FEMA to make grants for the purpose of providing a system of emergency preparedness for the protection of life and property in the United States from hazards and to vest responsibility for emergency preparedness jointly in the federal government and the states and their political subdivisions.

The federal government, through the EMPG Program, provides necessary direction, coordination, and guidance, and provides necessary assistance, as authorized in this title so that a comprehensive emergency preparedness system exists for all hazards. For more information, visit www.fema.gov/government/grant/empg.

Fire Management Assistance Grant Program

Fire Management Assistance is available to state, local and tribal governments, for the mitigation, management, and control of fires on publicly or privately owned forests or grasslands, which threaten such destruction as would constitute a major disaster.

The Fire Management Assistance declaration process is initiated when a State submits a request for assistance to the FEMA Regional Director at the time a "threat of major disaster" exists. The entire process is accomplished on an expedited basis and a FEMA decision is rendered in a matter of hours. For more information, visit the website at www.fema.gov/government/grant/fmagp/index.shtm.

Fire Prevention & Safety Grants (FP&S)

The Fire Prevention and Safety Grants (FP&S) are part of the Assistance to Firefighters Grants (AFG), and are under the purview of the Grant Programs Directorate in the Federal Emergency Management Agency. FP&S Grants support projects that enhance the safety of public and firefighters from fire and related hazards. The primary goal is to target high-risk populations and reduce injury and prevent death.

In 2005, Congress reauthorized funding for FP&S and expanded the eligible uses of funds to include Firefighter Safety Research and Development. For more information, visit the website at www.fema.gov/firegrants/fpsgrants/index.shtm.

Flood Mitigation Assistance Program

The FMA program was created as part of the National Flood Insurance Reform Act (NFIRA) of 1994 (42 U.S.C. 4101) with the goal of reducing or eliminating claims under the National Flood Insurance Program (NFIP). FEMA provides FMA funds to assist states and communities implement measures that reduce or eliminate the long-term risk of flood damage to buildings, manufactured homes, and other structures insured under the National Flood Insurance Program. For more information, visit the website at www.fema.gov/government/grant/fma/index.shtm.

Hazard Mitigation Grant Program (HMGP)

The Hazard Mitigation Grant Program (HMGP) provides grants to States and local governments to implement long-term hazard mitigation measures after a major disaster declaration. The purpose of the HMGP is to reduce the loss of life and property due to natural disasters and to enable mitigation measures to be implemented during the immediate recovery from a disaster. The HMGP is authorized under Section 404 of the Robert T. Stafford Disaster Relief and Emergency Assistance Act. For more information, visit the website at www.fema.gov/government/grant/hmgp/index.shtm.

Homeland Security Grant Program (HSGP)

The Homeland Security Grant Program provides a primary funding mechanism for building and sustaining national preparedness capabilities. HSGP is comprised of three interconnected grant programs: State Homeland Security Program (SHSP), Urban Areas Security Initiative (UASI), and Operation Stonegarden (OPSG). For more information visit www.fema.gov/government/grant/hsgp/index.shtm.

Pre-Disaster Mitigation Program (PDM)

The Pre-Disaster Mitigation (PDM) program provides funds to states, territories, tribal governments, communities, and universities for hazard mitigation planning and the implementation of mitigation projects prior to a disaster event. Funding these plans and projects reduces overall risks to the population and structures, while also reducing reliance on funding from actual disaster declarations.

PDM grants are to be awarded on a competitive basis and without reference to state allocations, quotas, or other formula-based allocation of funds. For more information visit the website at www.fema.gov/government/grant/pdm/index.shtm.

Public Assistance Grant Program (PA)

The mission of FEMA's Public Assistance (PA) Grant Program is to provide assistance to State, Tribal and local governments, and certain types of private non-profit organizations so that communities can quickly respond to and recover from major disasters or emergencies declared by the President.

Through the PA Program, FEMA provides supplemental federal disaster grant assistance for debris removal, emergency protective measures, and the repair, replacement, or restoration of disaster-damaged, publicly owned facilities and the facilities of certain Private Non-Profit (PNP) organizations. The PA Program also encourages protection of these damaged facilities from future events by providing assistance for hazard mitigation measures during the recovery process. For more information visit the website at www.fema.gov/government/grant/pa/index.shtm.

Reimbursement for Firefighting on Federal Property

Under Section 11 of the Federal Fire Prevention and Control Act of 1974, reimbursement may be made to fire departments for fighting fire on property owned by the federal government. Only firefighting costs over and above normal operating costs are reimbursable. Claims are submitted to USFA and are reviewed by the Deputy Administrator to ensure they meet the criteria outlined in the Code of Federal Regulations. For more information visit the website at www.usfa.fema.gov/fireservice/grants/rfff/.

Staffing For Adequate Fire & Emergency Response Grants (SAFER)

The Staffing for Adequate Fire and Emergency Response Grants (SAFER) was created to provide funding directly to fire departments and volunteer firefighter interest organizations to increase the number of trained, "front line" firefighters available in their communities.

The goal of SAFER is to enhance the local fire departments' abilities to comply with staffing, response, and operational standards established by the NFPA and OSHA (NFPA 1710 and/or NFPA 1720 and OSHA 1910.134). For more information, visit the website at www.fema.gov/firegrants/safer/index.shtm.

Tribal Homeland Security Grant Program (THSGP)

THSGP provides supplemental funding directly to eligible tribes to help strengthen the nation against risks associated with potential terrorist attacks. The THSGP enhances the ability of tribal nations to prevent, protect against, respond to, and recover from potential terrorist attacks and other hazards.

Pursuant to the 9/11 Commission Act, a directly eligible tribe applying for a grant shall designate an individual to serve as a tribal liaison with the Department of Homeland Security (DHS) and other federal, state, local, and regional government officials. The THSGP is an important part of the Administration's larger, coordinated effort to strengthen homeland security preparedness by including tribal nations. The THSGP implements objectives addressed in a series of post-9/11 laws, strategy plans, and Homeland Security Presidential Directives. For more information visit the website at http://www.fema.gov/government/grant/thsgp/index.shtm.

Private Sector and Community Engagement

FEMA Industry Liaison Program
The FEMA Industry Liaison Program is a point-of-entry for vendors seeking information on how to do business with FEMA during disasters and non-disaster periods of activity. The program coordinates vendor presentation meetings between vendors and FEMA program offices, establishes strategic relationships with vendor-supporting industry partners and stakeholders, coordinates Industry Days, conducts market research, responds to informal Congressional requests, and performs vendor analysis reporting.

Vendors interested in doing business with FEMA should take the following steps: Register in the Central Contractor Registration (CCR) at www.ccr.gov, contact the FEMA Industry Liaison Program at http://www.fema.gov/privatesector/industry/index.shtm, or call the Industry Liaison Support Center at (202) 646-1895.

FEMA Small Business Industry Liaison Program
The FEMA Small Business Industry Liaison Program provides information on doing business with FEMA, specifically with regard to small businesses. Small business vendors are routed to the FEMA Small Business Analyst for notification, support and processing. For more information see http://www.fema.gov/privatesector/industry/about.shtm or contact FEMA-SB@dhs.gov.

Office of Small and Disadvantaged Business Utilization (OSDBU)
The Office of Small and Disadvantaged Business Utilization operates within the Office of the Chief Procurement Officer and serves as the focal point for small business acquisition matters, and works closely with all DHS components to implement the program. OSDBU makes available forecasts of contract opportunities, vendor outreach sessions, a list of component small business specialists, DHS prime contractors, and information about the DHS mentor-protégé program.
For more information, see http://www.dhs.gov/openforbusiness or contact OSDBU at (202) 447-5555.

Research and Product Development

CBP Laboratories and Scientific Services
CBP Laboratories and Scientific Services coordinates technical and scientific support to all CBP trade and border protection activities. For more information, visit http://www.cbp.gov/xp/cgov/trade/automated/labs_scientific_svcs/.

Defense Technology Experimental Research (DETER)
DETER is a national cybersecurity experimental infrastructure which enables users to study and evaluate a wide range of computer security technologies including encryption, pattern detection, intrusion tolerant storage protocols, next generation network simulations, as well as develop and share educational material and tools to train the next generation of cyber-security experts.

Newsletters, published papers, videos and presentations can be viewed at http://www.isi.edu/deter/. Contact testbed-ops@isi.deterlab.net for more information.

DHS Small Business Innovation Research (SBIR) Program
The SBIR Program is designed to stimulate technological innovation, to strengthen the role of small business in meeting DHS research and development needs, to foster and encourage participation of socially and economically disadvantaged persons and women-owned small business concerns in technological innovation, and to increase the commercial application of DHS-supported research or research and development results.

SBIR research areas are chosen for their applicability to homeland security missions and address the needs of the seven DHS operational units. Additional information can be found at https://sbir2.st.dhs.gov.

DHS Technology Transfer Program
The Technology Transfer Program promotes the transfer and/or exchange of technology with industry, State and local governments, academia, and other federal agencies. The technologies developed and evaluated within DHS can have potential commercial applications and dramatically enhance the competitiveness of individual small businesses as well as expand areas of cooperation for non-federal partners. For more information, visit www.dhs.gov/xabout/structure/gc_1264538499667.shtm.

Homeland Open Security Technologies
Homeland Open Security Technologies works to improve federal, state, and local government's ability to collaborate with the open source software communities focused on security. The objectives are to improve the process for government acquisition of open technology, encourage the contribution of government funded research to these communities, and identify and seed development in prioritized gaps. For more information, see www.cyber.st.dhs.gov/host.html.

Mass Transit Security Technology Testing

In coordination with TSA's Office of Security Capabilities and DHS's Office of Science and Technology, the Mass Transit Division pursues development of multiple technologies to advance capabilities to detect and deter terrorist activity and prevent attacks.

TSA partners with mass transit and passenger rail agencies to conduct pilot testing of various security technologies. These activities evaluate capabilities in the varied operational environments that prevail in rail and bus operations across the country.

For more information, contact MassTransitSecurity@dhs.gov.

Minority Serving Institutions (MSIs) Programs

MSI Programs include the Scientific Leadership Award (SLA) grant program and the Summer Research Team program. Both programs improve the capabilities of MSIs to conduct research, education, and training in areas critical to homeland security and to develop a new generation of scientists capable of advancing homeland security goals. The SLA program provides three to five years of institutional support for students and early career faculty. The Summer Research Team programs provide support for a ten-week collaborative research experience between recipient MSIs and the Centers of Excellence.

For more information, please visit Historical Funding Opportunity Announcements (CDG and SLA) at http://grants.gov/; DHS Scholars Program at http://www.orau.gov/dhsed/; or Summer Research Team Program at http://www.orau.gov/dhseducation/. For more information, please contact universityprograms@hq.dhs.gov.

National Urban Security Technology Laboratory

The NUSTL tests, evaluates, and analyzes homeland security capabilities while serving as a technical authority to first responder, State, and local entities. NUSTL is a federal technical resource supporting the successful development, integration, and transition of homeland security technologies into operational end-user environments.

NUSTL's broad ranging relationships with the homeland security community enable the use of the New York metropolitan area as an urban test location for the diverse technologies and systems being developed to prepare and protect our nation. For more information, contact nustl@dhs.gov.

Appendix A

Department of Homeland Security Contacts

COMPONENTS	POC	Email	Phone Numbers
CBP	CBP State, Local, Tribal Liaison	CBP-STATE-LOCAL-TRIBAL-LIAISON@cbp.dhs.gov	(202) 325-0775
CBP	ACE Help Desk	-	(800) 927-8729
CBP	Air & Marine Operations Center (AMOC)		(951) 656-8000
CBP	Carrier Liaison Program	clp@dhs.gov	(202) 344-3440
CBP	CBP INFO Center	https://help.cbp/app/home	(877) CBP-5511
CBP	Client Representative Office	-	(571) 468-5000
CBP	Electronic System for Travel Authorization (ESTA)	https://esta.cbp.dhs.gov/esta/	(202) 344-3710
CBP	Global Entry	cbp.goes.support@dhs.gov	(866) 530-4172
CBP	Industry Partnership Program	industry.partnership@dhs.gov	(202) 344-1180
CBP	Intellectual Property Rights Help Desk	ipr.helpdesk@dhs.gov	(562) 980-3119 ext. 252
CBP	Intellectual Property Rights Policy and Programs	iprpolicyprograms@dhs.gov	
CBP	National Gang Intelligence Center	-	(703) 414-8600
CBP	Private Aircraft Travel Entry Programs	private.aircraft.support@dhs.gov	
CBP	Secure Freight Initiative	securefreightinitiative@dhs.gov	
CBP	Trusted Traveler Programs (NEXUS, SENTRI, FAST)	cbp.goes.support@dhs.gov	
CRCL	Disability Preparedness	Disability.preparedness@dhs.gov	(202) 357-8483
CRCL	Training	crcltraining@dhs.gov	(202) 357-8258
CRCL	Tanya Cantrell	Tanya.Cantrell@dhs.gov	(202) 254-8214
NPPD/CS&C	Control Systems Security Program (CSSP)	CSSP@dhs.gov	
NPPD/CS&C	Cybersecurity Evaluation Tool	CSET@dhs.gov	
NPPD/CS&C	Information Technology Sector	ncsd_cipcs@hq.dhs.gov	
NPPD/CS&C	Office of Emergency Communications	oec@hq.dhs.gov	
NPPD/CS&C	Software Assurance Program	software.assurance@dhs.gov	
NPPD/CS&C	U.S. Computer Emergency Readiness Team (US-CERT	info@us-cert.gov	(888) 282-0870
NPPD/CS&C	US-CERT Secure Operations Center	soc@us-cert.gov	(888) 282-0878
NPPD/CS&C	State, Local, Tribal and Territorial Cybersecurity Engagement Program	CSC_SLTT@hq.dhs.gov	
DHS	Center for faith-based and Neighborhood Partnerships	infofbci@dhs.gov	
DHS	Homeland Security Information Network (HSIN)	hsin.helpdesk@dhs.gov	(866) 430-0162
DHS	Lessons Learned and Information Sharing (LLIS)	feedback@llis.dhs.gov	(866) 276-7001
DHS	National Information Exchange Model Program	niempmo@niem.gov	

DHS	Office of Intergovernmental Affairs (IGA)	Dhs.iga@hq.dhs.gov	(202) 282-9310
DNDO	Steven Gunnink	D.Gunnink@hq.dhs.gov	(202) 254-7106
FEMA	Richard Flores	richard.flores@dhs.gov	(202) 646-4663
FLETC	Terry Todd	terry.todd@dhs.gov	(575) 746-5717
I&A	Fusion Center Support	FusionCenterSupport@hq.dhs.gov	(202) 447-4242
ICE	Lorena Balanta	Lorena.balanta@dhs.gov	(202) 732-3925
NPPD/IP	Renee Murphy	Renee.Murphy@hq.dhs.gov	(703) 603-5083
OGC	Randy Kaplan	Randall.Kaplan@hq.dhs.gov	(202) 282-9941
OHA	Tamara Blount	Tamara.Blount@hq.dhs.gov	(202) 254-6855
OPS	Denzil D. Thies	denzil.thies@hq.dhs.gov	(202) 357-7622
PRIV	Ken Hunt	ken.hunt@hq.dhs.gov	(703) 235-0762
S&T	Stephanie Willett	Stephanie.willett@hq.dhs.gov	(202) 658-8229
TSA	Howard Goldman	Howard.Goldman@dhs.gov	(571) 227-2679
USCG	Kirstin Riesbeck	Kirstin.riesbeck@uscg.mil	(202) 245-0527
USCIS	Mary Flores	Mary.F.Flores@uscis.dhs.gov	(202) 272-8258

www.ingramcontent.com/pod-product-compliance
Lightning Source LLC
Chambersburg PA
CBHW052011280526
45793CB00005B/938